INSIDER
SECRETS
TO
KILLER
TRAVEL
DEALS

LARRY GELWIX

Columbus Companies
P.O. Box 22617
Salt Lake City, UT 84122-2617
Telephone: 801-295-9568
Fax: 801-295-9688

Library of Congress Cataloging-in-Publication Data Pending

ISBN 1-890107-01-8

To my wife, Cathy, whose love and support
make my travel adventures and global wandering possible;
and to my children Larry, Emily,
Jennifer, Sara, and Keaton,
who love to travel almost as much as
their Dad does!

I express my appreciation and gratitude to
Danica E. Duran, Whitney Davis, and Juli H. Wells
for their help in publishing this book.
Many thanks to my partner Mark Faldmo
for his friendship and encouragement.

Introduction

I love to travel. Pure and simple. For me, traveling is a passion! I think I'm the luckiest guy in the world. I've traveled the world and seen just about every corner of the globe several times over. I've crisscrossed this country more times than I can count; traveled throughout North America, South America, and the Caribbean; and trekked glaciers and remote mountain wilderness areas. I've hiked the Inca trails of Peru and Machu Picchu, lived with an Aboriginal tribe in the Outback of Australia, scuba dived the Great Barrier Reef, thrilled at the splendors of Western and Eastern Europe, climbed inside and through the pyramid tunnels of Egypt, walked the ancient streets of Jerusalem, sailed and paddled by canoe throughout Polynesia, traveled through India by train and bicycle, visited the temples and wonders of China and Southeast Asia, and thrilled at the serenity of an African night! In short, my life has been a travel odyssey of adventure and excitement.

For most, travel is both exciting and challenging. It is full of adventure, but can also be full of uncertainty and questions. Vacation travelers dream of far away places and sun-drenched beaches. Business travelers dream of on-time airplanes, no itinerary surprises, and the seat next to them remaining unoccupied. Both the leisure and business traveler share one common dream: To get the best travel deal! Few things in life ruin a trip more than knowing the guy next to you on *exactly* the same flight, itinerary, cruise, hotel room, etc. paid less, maybe hundreds or thousands of dollars less, than you!

I love a challenge! Finding the best value and the lowest price is a game to me! It's not luck and it's not by chance. Buying travel and finding the best value is not exclusively the result of hard work, but comes as a result of *smart work!* Savvy travelers know how to **Shop Smart!** The purpose of this book is to share a lifetime of insider travel secrets and knowledge. This book is not intended to be exhaustive (that may come later), but to steer you in the right direction and to help you ask the right questions. Here are two guarantees I can make. First, what you learn in this book *will* (not maybe) save you hundreds and thousands of dollars off of regular travel rates....if you follow my advice. I guarantee it. Absolutely, positively, period, final, and without hesitation! Second, the travel industry is dynamic and constantly changing. You need an advocate on *your* side, protecting *your* wallet, and keeping *you* informed. *Insider Secrets To Killer Travel Deals* will start you down the road to travel savings. As an update to the information in this book, join me on the ***Travel Show***, broadcast coast-to-coast on 128 radio stations. As host of the program, I keep listeners on top of what's hot and what's not; where the best buys, discount offers, and promotions are; and how to reduce the cost of travel. For a list of stations that carry the ***Travel Show***, contact Columbus Broadcasting Network at 801-296-6847 or fax 801-295-9688.

The information in this book is accurate as it goes to press. Travel is in a constant state of change. The savings strategies reviewed are constant, but all offers contain expiration dates and are subject to change without notice by the airlines, cruise lines, hotels, tour operators, and car rental companies. What never changes is this....that the deals just keep coming! We will discover the creative art of saving big money on your airfare, cruises, hotels, and car rentals. You *can* save hundreds, even thousands of dollars on your travel! You *will* save if you apply the insider travel secrets I teach you. So climb aboard the ***Discount Express,*** and learn how to ***Shop Smart!***

Table of Contents

Chapter 1 - Travel Deals Are Everywhere...3

Chapter 2 - Talk The Talk...7

Chapter 3 - Airline Tickets: Don't Get Taken For A Ride...................14
    Plan Ahead..14
    Be Flexible...14
    Fare Wars...18
    Promotions and Discount Coupons...........................20
    Consolidators..22
    Alternate Cities...24
    Back -To-Back Ticketing...28
    Breaking Fares..30
    Point Beyond Fares..32
    Buy a Lower Priced Round-Trip Ticket,
        even when you only need a one-way ticket.........33
    International Airline Passes...33
    Special Circumstance Travel.......................................36
    Children...36
    Student and Youth Fares..38
    Credit Card and Frequent Flyer Awards....................40
    Internet and Last-Minute Sales...................................47
    Creative Airline Ticket Summary...............................50

Chapter 4 - Travel Clubs...53
    Three Types of Travel Clubs.......................................53
    Good Travel Bargains..57
    Travel Club Checklist..59

Chapter 5 - Cruises: Don't Get Soaked...63
    Shop Smart: Steps to Buying a Cruise...................64
    How to Get the Best Cruise Fare.................................69
    Pre- and Post-Cruise Stays..73
    Freighter Cruises...73

Chapter 6 - Hotels: How To Avoid A Nightmare!..................................77
    Hotel *Shop Smart*...80
    Discount Books...81
    Special Affinity Offers..84
    Little Known Accommodations...................................85

Chapter 7 - Car Rentals: How Not To Crash!..89
    Discount Rates..89
    CDW: Collision Damage Waiver................................91
    International Rentals...92

Chapter 8 - Senior Citizen Discounts: Golden Rates In The Golden Years............97
          Associations...98
          Airline Discounts...99
          Rental Car Discounts..104
          Hotel Discounts...104
          National Parks..105
          Train Discounts..106

Chapter 9 - Trains: Riding The Rails...109
          Amtrak..109
          Steam Trains...110
          European Trains, Rail Passes, and Tickets............................110
          Trains in Great Britain...113
          Eurobus..115
          Japan Rail Pass...116

Chapter 10 - How To Travel And Get Paid To Do It!....................................117
          Free and Paid Vacations...117
          Cruise Free...118
          Fly, Tour, and Stay Free..118

Chapter 11 - Courier Travel: Get Ready, Get Set, Go. . . Today!...........................125

Chapter 12 - Just A Little Fun Stuff!..133

Epilogue..150

Appendix 1 - Airline Frequent Flyer Programs With Airline,
          Hotel, And Car Rental Partners...151

Appendix 2 - Frequent Lodging Programs..165

Appendix 3 - Tourist And Visitor Information Offices...167

Appendix 4 - Rail Companies...173

Appendix 5 - Helpful Telephone Numbers...177

Appendix 6 - Recommended Reading..183

Chapter 1

Travel Deals Are Everywhere

There are so many travel deals, even *"Killer* Travel Deals!" It's amazing how many people throw their money away. (I guess the polite phrase would be they spend more than is necessary.) Maybe they're just good folks who want to help out corporate America? (Not!) Actually, they just don't know what discount deals are available. There is no shortage of people who want to save money and even travel for free. There is no shortage of legitimate travel offers and programs that will provide significant savings and even free travel. There is, however, a shortage of information on where these deals are and how to take advantage of them.

Here are just a few (just enough to wet your appetite) of the killer travel deals that are available to those who *Shop Smart.* There is a tidal wave of bargains from airlines, cruise lines, hotels, tour operators, and car rental companies who are locked in fierce competition for your business and travel dollars. All of these offers are currently valid or have been available recently. How many did you know about?

- **Free ticket** on Northwest Airlines for spending $25 per month in long-distance calls.
- **Free ticket** on Delta Air Lines for buying furniture from Thomasville.
- **Free ticket** to any of the 53 cities served by Austrian Airlines in Europe, the Middle East, or Africa.
- **Free ticket** on Air South. Fly three round-trips and receive a free ticket.
- **Free ticket** in the 48 states when you buy a trans-Atlantic ticket on British Airways.
- **Free ticket** on Aeromexico. Buy one ticket to Acapulco, Ixtapa, Cabo, or Puerto Vallarta and receive a FREE ticket anywhere Aeromexico flies in Mexico.

- **Free ticket to Hawaii** when you book seven-night hotel accommodations.
- **Free ticket** on Delta Shuttle. Children fly free with an adult between Boston, New York City, and Washington, D.C.
- **Free intra-Europe ticket** when you fly Aer Lingus trans-Atlantic.
- **Free companion ticket** to London for buying a $55 golf starter kit.
- **Free companion ticket** to London for buying five pair of boxer shorts. (Really!)
- **Free companion ticket** on Delta, American, or America West for buying a box of 12 golf balls.
- **Buy one, get one free** anywhere Delta flies in the world for spending $30 on computer software.
- **Buy one, get one free** on American Airlines when you are approved for a VISA card.
- **Buy one, get one free** on TWA for using your MasterCard.
- **Buy one, get one free** on 10 major airlines when using your American Express card.
- **Buy one, get one free** to Mexico for enrolling (no cost) in Aeromexico's frequent flyer program.
- **Buy one, get one free** on inter-island flights in Hawaii on Aloha Airlines for purchasing $40 in groceries.
- **Buy One, Get One Free** to any one of six South American cities served by Aeroperu, plus get a **free ticket** to any city in Peru.
- **Buy one, get one free** on America West, Delta, and Southwest.
- **Buy one, get one free** on Amtrak.
- **Free upgrade to First Class and a $99 companion ticket** on Delta just for answering a short travel survey. Survey takes about 60 seconds to fill out.
- **20% Delta Air Lines discount** for the family when you enroll your children in the airline's Fantastic Flyer program. Enrollment is free.
- **25% Air New Zealand discount** on Business Class fares to Sydney and Auckland.
- **50% discount on USAir to West Palm Beach.** Call the Palm Beach County Visitors Bureau and ask for a FREE discount coupon.
- **$100 discount** on Continental Airlines simply for processing a roll of film.
- **$100 discount** on TWA for renting a car from Alamo.
- **$99 round-trip airfare on Delta** for two children ages 2-11 for buying $30 worth of toys.
- **Up to 70% discount** on Northwest Airlines with a $50 grocery purchase.
- **Free car days** from Alamo if you ask for the right promotion.

- **$9.99 per day car rental.**
- **Special, unpublished fares** on USAir for buying $50 of groceries. These fares are not available to the general public.
- **$149 Companion Fare** anywhere in the 48 states on Northwest Airlines.
- **$129 Companion Fare** on Northwest Airlines for charging your tickets on Diners Club.
- **Free 3-day/2-night resort stay.** No tricks. No gimmicks. (For real!) And you don't need to win any contest. I checked this one out myself.
- **Save 70% on hotels.** This is *so-o-o* easy.
- **Special hotel "code words"** that qualify you for rock bottom room rates.
- **Orlando and Disney World.** Large suite, that sleeps six, with a full kitchen and separate bedroom for only **$49 per night.** Not per person, but per room, per night. There's more. FREE breakfast, lunch, and dinner for children under 12; one FREE adult admission to Watermania and Cypress Gardens; and a coupon book worth up to $300 in savings at local area restaurants, stores, and attractions.
- **Cruise lines award free cabins on almost every cruise.** Do you know how to qualify?
- **Cruise a family of four.** One-week Caribbean cruise from $212 per person. No kidding!
- **40-70% discount on cruises.** Most major cruise lines. Thousands of cruise dates and departures.
- **Children cruise FREE.**
- **Friends cruise FREE.** Which cruise lines and departures allow you to bring along a friend or two for FREE?
- **Cruise "code words"** that unlock deep discounts.
- **Double and triple frequent flyer miles.**
- **How to earn frequent flyer mileage points** on almost everything you buy, including your home mortgage and charitable donations!
- **Travel FREE and get paid to do it.** Serious offer. I have told tens of thousands of people how to do it. It's easy and it's fun! It's unlike *anything* you have ever heard of before. No selling. Nothing to buy. No group travel. You can travel alone, with a companion, or with your family. No special training. Thousands of people have done it and come back year after year. I'm absolutely serious!
- **Savings Strategies:** you will see a long list of them in this book. Have you ever heard of "creative ticketing?" Back-to-back ticketing? Alternate city ticketing? Double dip discounts? Breaking fares? The list goes on and on.

These offers are only a drop in the bucket of the travel deals available. Why don't more people take advantage of these deals? Simple. They don't know about them. Did you?

Wouldn't it be easy if there was a single price for an airline ticket, cruise, car rental, or hotel room? It would be so simple, I would be out of a job! No worries, however, it will never happen. It only seems to get *more* confusing. Understand this, airlines, cruise lines, hotels, and car rental companies want to get as high a rate as possible. They would be happy if you paid twice what you do now. That's capitalism. Conversely, I want to pay as little as I can and still receive value. This is one of Larry's Laws: Shop value, not just price!

The following chapters will provide the insider secrets of how to **Shop Smart** and get **Killer Travel Deals!**

Chapter 2
Talk The Talk!

KNOW THE LINGO. Understand basic travel terminology and language. Did you know that a direct flight is not necessarily a non-stop flight? Direct means that although the plane may stop en route, passengers need not change aircraft. Non-stop means no stops. Here are a few terms you should know:

ADA room: Hotel room that complies with the requirements of the Americans With Disabilities Act. Also referred to as Special Needs Accommodations.

Add-on fare: A fare added on to your international ticket to get you from your home city to the gateway city.

Airport Code: Three-letter code that identifies an airport. For example, San Francisco is SFO; Miami is MIA; Chicago/O'Hare is ORD; and Frankfurt, Germany is FRA. Always check your luggage tags. Your final destination airport code should be listed on the tag.

American Plan (AP): A hotel rate, also referred to as "full board," which includes a room and three meals daily. Referred to in Europe as "full pension."

APEX: Advance Purchase Excursion Fare. One of the lowest international priced fares.

ATO: Airport Ticket Office. Airline ticketing at the airport counter.

Airline Affinity Card: Credit card that awards frequent flyer miles for every dollar you spend regardless of what the purchase is for.

Back-to-back ticketing: Buying two discounted, restricted round-trip tickets and using half of each, instead a one unrestricted ticket when the cost of the two tickets is less than the higher priced unrestricted ticket.

Blackout dates: Dates when promotions and special fares are not valid, usually during the holidays or other high demand travel days.

Boarding pass: A card that will allow a passenger to board a flight or cruise. The boarding pass, which may be different from your ticket, identifies your seat or cabin assignment.

Breaking the fare: Issuing two or more tickets in order to reduce the fare. For example, the lowest fare from City A to City C is $400. Fly from City A to City B for $100 and from City B to City C for $200. New ticket cost is $300. Savings is $100. In many cases, you will fly the very same planes as the $400 itinerary, but have a lower fare. This practice is also known as "split ticketing."

Bulk fare: Special fare negotiated by a tour operator or travel agency that buys tickets in a large or "bulk" quantity. The tickets are re-sold at rates lower than published fares.

Bulkhead: A seat or row directly behind a cabin wall in an airplane.

Bumping: A passenger with a ticket and confirmed reservation is denied boarding of his/her flight, usually because the airline has taken more reservations than there are available seats. There is voluntary and involuntary bumping, officially known as "Denied Boarding."

Business Class: Special section of an aircraft with many in-flight enhancements. The seating, service and amenities are much better than Coach Class, but not as upscale as First Class.

Cancellation penalty: Penalty for canceling a ticket, cruise, or tour.

Capacity controlled: The number and availability of discount seats, rooms, cabins, or cars is limited.

CDW: Collision Damage Waiver. Erroneously called rental car "insurance." CDW is a waiver of liability for damage to your rental car.

City pair: The cities from which you depart and arrive, or your origin and destination.

Coach Class: Any seat in the coach or economy section of the plane.

Coach Fare: Can mean two very different things. Coach fare can mean "full coach fare" also known as a "Y" fare. I call this the "OUCH" fare. Absolutely outrageously high priced fares. Those who pay this rate usually have to travel ASAP and have little or no flexibility. It can be as much as five or six times more than the discounted coach fares. In some cases, "Coach Fare" can also refer to *any* fare that seats you in the coach or economy section of the plane, including discount fares.

Code share: One airplane with two or more airlines sharing the same flight. Both sell space on it.

Commuter carrier: Usually a regional carrier. The government defines a commuter carrier as one whose aircraft seats 62 or fewer passengers. This usually, but not always, means a prop (propeller, not jet) aircraft.

Companion Fare: The first passenger buys a qualifying fare and a second passenger on the same itinerary goes free or at a reduced rate.

Concierge: A good person to know! An individual at the hotel who will answer your questions and assist you with special requests.

Configuration: The seating arrangement on an airplane. For example, a Boeing 767 is usually configured with a row of two seats, an aisle, a row of three seats, an aisle, and a row of two seats. This configuration is referred to as "2-3-2."

Connection: A change of planes before reaching your final destination.

Consolidator: Ticket company that contracts and/or buys airline tickets, hotel rooms, and/or cruises at substantial discounts and re-sells the tickets, rooms, or cruises usually at a rate below the lowest published rates.

Continental breakfast: Light breakfast, usually consisting of rolls, toast, coffee, and juice.

Continental Plan: A hotel rate that includes the room and continental breakfast.

Corporate rate: A discounted hotel rate usually offered to business travelers.

CRS: Computer Reservation System. A computer network through which travel services and products are booked.

CTO: City Ticket Office of an airline.

Debit memo: An airline demand notice sent to a travel agency alleging additional monies owed to the airline. A debit memo is usually connected with a previously issued ticket where the airline believes a ticketing error occured. Debit memos are to travel agents what a cross is to Dracula!

Denied boarding: The official term for "bumping." You have a confirmed reservation and ticket, but you are denied travel on that flight, usually because of an oversell (more passengers with tickets than available seats). There is involuntary and voluntary denied boarding.
Involuntary denied boarding: You did not volunteer, but have been "bumped" against your will. Ask for a complete copy of the airline's denied boarding policy. You may be entitled to cash, free travel, hotel, phone calls, and meals — plus accommodations on the next available flight.
Voluntary denied boarding: The aircraft is in an "oversell" and will ask for "volunteers" to give up their seat in exchange for compensation at the airline's discretion, usually in the form of free future travel. If there are more volunteers than needed seats, whatever the airline offers is what you can get. If they are short on volunteers, negotiate! Up the ante! If your time is flexible, you may wait for a later flight and get a free ticket for future travel. Not a bad deal!

Denied boarding compensation: Also known as **DBC.** Compensation given to you by an airline when they have "bumped" you. Involuntary DBC is covered by government regulations. Voluntary DBC is solely at the discretion of the airline. In an involuntary denied boarding situation, airlines rarely, if ever, will fully notify you of your rights. Ask for a written statement of your DBC rights. Airlines are required to make a copy available to you.

Direct flight: Your plane will stop one or more times before reaching your final destination. Direct does not mean non-stop. It means no change of planes or connections en route.

Double booking: Making two or more reservations for the same person at different times. Some business travelers do this when they don't know their schedule. This is why airlines, hotels, and car rental companies "overbook" their flights, hotels, and cars. Travel suppliers hate this practice and rightly so. It ties up their inventory. Also known as a "dupe."

Double occupancy: Two persons sharing the same room or accommodations. The double occupancy rate is usually shown as a per person rate, based upon two persons sharing the room or cruise cabin.

Down line: All future segments of an itinerary.

Drop-off fee: A fee imposed by car rental companies when you pick-up the car in one city and return it to a different city.

European Plan (EP): Hotel rate that pays for the room only and no meals.

Excursion fare: A discounted fare that carries various restrictions, usually advance purchase and minimum/maximum stay requirements.

Fare basis: An alpha numeric code that identifies the type of ticket you have purchased and the applicable rules governing the usage of that ticket. This code is listed in the CRS and is printed on your airline ticket. Learn how to identify it. Also known as "Fare Basis Code."

FIM: Flight Interruption Manifest. When an airline cannot take you as planned, they "FIM" you to another airline who will fly you to your destination.

FIT: Any independent travel plans. Originally it was an acronym for "Foreign Independent Travel" and DIT was "Domestic Independent Travel." Now the term "FIT" is used to describe any travel taken independent of a tour group, also known as "Free Independent Travel."

Frequent Flyer program: A program that awards points for the miles you travel and/or purchases you make on the sponsoring airline and its program partners. Points can be redeemed for free travel and merchandise.

Gate agent: Airline agent working at the arrival or departure gate.

Gateway city: The city from which your international flight departs.

Hidden-city ticketing: See "point beyond fares."

Hub: A city which enjoys a concentration of an airline's flights. It serves as a connecting point for passengers. For example, Dallas is a hub for American Airlines and Delta Air Lines. Chicago is a hub for United Airlines. London is a hub for British Airways.

Hub and Spoke: An airline industry term for a city which serves as a hub for an airline and where passengers are routed to take connecting flights to their final destination. The "hub" is the airport that flights bring passengers to, not necessarily being their final destination. The "spoke" is a connecting flight that flies passengers to their final destination.

Incentive travel: Travel that is used as an incentive or reward to individuals, usually company employees or customers.

Inclusive rate: Hotel or resort rate that includes your room, meals, and activities.

Interline agreement: A reciprocal agreement between two airlines. Such an agreement means that both carriers will cooperate on services. An "interline ticketing agreement" means that each carrier will accept tickets validated or issued by the other. An "interline luggage agreement" means that carriers will exchange passenger luggage without the passenger being forced to retrieve it from each airline and re-check it at each stop. Not all airlines offer interline agreements.

Interline connection: You will change airlines. For example, you fly from Dallas to Los Angeles on Delta and then change planes and fly to Auckland on Air New Zealand. This is an "interline" connection.

Joint fare: A single fare offered jointly by two or more airlines on which you will fly to complete your journey.

Leg: A segment of your flight itinerary.

Load factor: The number of airline seats sold as a percentage of the total seats available. For example, a 75% load factor means 75% of the available seats are filled.

Manifest: An official list of passengers on an airplane or cruise ship.

Meeting fare/rate: Discount given by an airline or hotel to a meeting, convention, or conference.

Midweek (X): In most cases, this refers to travel Monday through Thursday inclusive.

Modified American Plan (MAP): Hotel rate that includes your room, breakfast, and one other meal. Referred to in Europe as "half-board," "demi-pension," and/or "half-pension."

No show: A passenger who fails to show-up for a confirmed reservation.

Occupancy rate: The percentage of hotel rooms that are occupied.

Open jaw: Term for when you fly into one city and return home from another. For example, you fly from Dallas to New York City, get yourself to Boston and fly home to Dallas from Boston. This is an Open Jaw. A *Double Open Jaw* is when you fly from City A to City B, get yourself to City C and fly back to City D. In our example, you fly from Dallas to New York City, then fly from Boston back to Houston. This is a Double Open Jaw.

Option date: A deadline by which a deposit and/or payment must be made or your reservation may be canceled.

Overbooking: A travel supplier (airline, hotel, car rental company, etc.) takes more reservations than available capacity in expectation of cancellations.

PAI: Personal Accident Insurance.

PEC: Personal Effects Coverage.

PFC: Passenger Facility Charge. Nice term for another goverment tax, usually $3 per airport. This is in addition to your ticket price.

Pitch: The distance from one point, such as the front of your seat cushion, to the exact same point on the seat in front of you.

PNR: Passenger Name Record. Fancy name for your airline reservation record.

Point beyond fare: You want to travel from City A to City B. You buy a ticket from City A to City C, which is less expensive than a ticket to City B, knowing that your flight stops in City B. You simply get off the plane in city B. Also known as "hidden-city" ticketing.

Positive space: A confirmed reservation.

Published fare: Any airline fare that is published and filed. It is available to the general public.

Rack rate: A full or "regular" hotel rate that has not been discounted.

Rebate: A travel agency returns or rebates a portion of their travel commisions to an account. Also known as "revenue sharing."

Restricted ticket: A ticket with restrictions or conditions. Common restrictions include no itinerary changes, non-refundable ("use it or lose it"), Saturday-night stay, minimum stay, maximum stay, day of travel, time of day, and so on.

Rule 240: Originally referred to the Civil Aeronautics Board (CAB) rule 240 which governed denied boarding compensation and passenger re-accommodation. The CAB was eliminated when air transportation and airlines were deregulated. Consequently, Rule 240 doesn't exist anymore, but the term is still used by airline employees when dealing with DBC and rerouting of passengers.

Run-of-House (ROH): Any room in a hotel.

Run-of-Ship (ROS): Any cabin or stateroom on a cruise ship.

Season: Airlines, hotels, and cruise lines divide the year into seasons for pricing purposes. Typical seasons include peak or high, shoulder or middle, and low, economy, or value.

Segment: A portion or "leg" of your trip.

Self catering: A room that includes a full or partial kitchen.

Single supplement: An additional charge or supplement for one person occupying a room or cruise cabin rather than two persons.

Split ticketing: See "breaking the fare."

Stand-by: You are "standing by" or waiting for a seat. You may or may not have a confirmed reservation. You must wait and hope a seat becomes available. You are "wait listed."

Supervisor: The agent(s) in charge at the airport. If you do not receive satisfaction from the counter or gate agent, ask to speak to the supervisor who may be authorized to grant waivers and "bend" the rules. Never shout or threaten. State your situation clearly and politely and ask for what you need. Honey attracts more bees than vinegar!

Through fare: The fare from one city to another.

Unpublished fare: A private deal or contract fare, not always available to the general public.

Unrestricted ticket: No restrictions or conditions on the ticket.

Upgrade: Moved from one class of service to another. For example, upgrade from Coach Class to First Class.

Value Added Tax: Government tax on goods and services. Commonly referred to as "V.A.T."

Wait list: Your reservation is not confirmed, but is subject to space becoming available. If your wait list "clears," it means you are now confirmed.

Waiver: Rules and/or conditions of your ticket purchase are "waived."

Weekend (W): In most cases, this refers to travel Friday through Sunday inclusive.

Chapter 3
Airline Tickets
Don't Get Taken For A Ride!

Can you make any sense of airline pricing? If you can, you're as crazy as the airlines! Each and every day there are over 200,000 airfare changes. These changes can be price, rules, advance purchase, minimum stay, maximum stay, and so on.

With so many changes, how does one find the rock bottom price? Easy! Learn to *Shop Smart!* I've never met an airfare I didn't try to chop down, and usually with some success!

Here are some of the best methods of reducing your airline ticket cost.

PLAN AHEAD. This is absolutely the best advice I can give. Whenever possible, plan ahead and don't put off your ticket purchase. The best fares usually require an advance purchase. Sometimes a last-minute purchase is unavoidable, but many times higher fares are due to negligence. It is a myth that the best deals are the last-minute sales. True, there are some good last-minute deals, but the vast majority of savings go to the early bird.

BE FLEXIBLE. This applies more to leisure and vacation travelers than to business travelers. Sometimes the business traveler simply cannot be flexible.

Not all flights from City A to City B are priced the same. Flights on the same airline, but at different times of the day or days of the week may offer a lower fare. Airlines frequently offer price incentives to attract passengers away from the busiest travel times. Ask your agent for alternate flights or airlines that may offer a lower price. Ask, "Would the fare be reduced if I went a day earlier or a day later or at another time of day?"

Here's an example. I took a call on my radio show from Carol in Cleveland. She wanted to visit her parents in West Palm Beach, Florida and wanted to leave on Sunday. The lowest published "through fare" between Cleveland and West Palm Beach with only a six-day advance purchase was $848 (OUCH fare!). By "Breaking the Fare" and issuing one ticket from Cleveland to Newark and another ticket from Newark to West Palm Beach, the fare was reduced to $438 with no change in her desired travel plans or travel days. Not a bad savings! There was no non-stop service between Cleveland and West Palm Beach, so she would have to make a connection (changing planes) regardless. The airlines (remember they want to get as high a fare as possible) would hardly suggest an alternative in order to save money. I asked if she could wait one day and fly Monday morning, instead of Sunday afternoon? She said she could, and then I dropped the bomb on her (no pun intended). Her round-trip fare was now only $198. Delta offered a special midweek excursion fare. Her flexibility saved her big time! She called the *Travel Show* and learned how to *Shop Smart!*

For unknown reasons, none of the airlines or travel agents Carol called offered her either alternative, viz., "Breaking the Fare," or waiting one day to save $650. Why?

What factors affect the price of a ticket? That's easy to answer. Whatever the market will bear. It's Econ 101 — Supply and Demand! Have you noticed fares where there is little or no competition? How about airfares over the Christmas holidays? Yep, the OUCH fare! Competition is the single biggest market factor driving airfares. Other factors include the day of the week (midweek is often less expensive than weekend), the time of day (off-peak hour flights are sometimes less costly), and the season of travel (many destinations have different prices for different months of the year).

FARE WARS. Airlines will cut their fares, sometimes drastically, to sell seats at "soft" times to stimulate travel or match competitors. This is one of the best travel bargains available. Fare wars are somewhat predictable. Domestic fare wars usually break out in January, mid-spring, early summer, late summer, and fall. I have charted the fare wars over the last few years and have detected a fairly regular pattern.

The best sources of information on fare wars are travel clubs that will fax you "hot" deals as they break, a travel agent who will call you the day a fare war breaks out, local and national newspapers, and, of course, the very best source is listening to the *Travel Show.*

Do some shopping. Not all airlines automatically match each others' fares anymore. The "lowest" fare on Airline A may be higher than the lowest fare on Airline B. For example, not long ago the lowest published fare from Salt Lake City to Washington, D.C. was $116 on Northwest, which was running a special. All other airlines were charging $460 (OUCH!). Other carriers chose not to match Northwest. If you had called any other airline and asked for their "absolutely, posivitely lowest fare between Salt Lake City and Washington, D.C.," you would have been correctly quoted $460. That was *their* lowest fare, but not *the* lowest fare. (You cannot expect one airline to give you costs and information on other airlines.) While most fare differences between airlines may not be as dramatic as this one, they are often substantial. It is a myth that all airlines automatically match other airlines' fares.

Act quickly, but not hastily. Most cheap fares require purchase within 24 hours of reservation. Make your reservation, but wait a day before actually purchasing the ticket. See what happens the next day after the fare war breaks out. Sometimes the fares drop again. Discount seats are limited and go quickly, so be prepared to act. Be advised, however, that in a few situations, the fare has actually gone up the next day. You are not guaranteed a price until you actually purchase your ticket. If you have a favorite destination, ask your travel agent to call you immediately whenever a "hot" deal comes up to that city.

Double Dip. Many fares offered during a fare war can be further reduced by using creative ticketing techniques and coupon/certificate discount offers. There is a flood of discount coupons on the market. Most offer $25-$100 off the lowest available domestic fare.[1] International coupons may offer additional discount savings. Never assume that just because the airlines are shooting at each other in a fare war, you can't get an even lower price. Now, this is when the game gets really exciting! Beat the airlines at fare pricing!

Did you miss the ticketing deadline? Airline tariffs or "fares" contain a ticketing deadline. The deadline is usually midnight on whatever day the fare expires. For example, if a fare requires ticketing by May 1, this means that you must purchase your ticket no later than midnight, May 1. (There may be other ticketing requirements also, but we're only dealing with the deadline here.)

Suppose you don't make the deadline and it's after midnight and you're kicking yourself for missing the deadline. Is there anything you can do? Maybe. If your local time is still within a few hours of midnight, call the airline's reservation number in another time zone. You can get that number by calling the airline where you live and asking them for an out-of-state reservation number. Or, call Directory Information for another area code and ask for the airline's reservation number there. During Daylight Savings Time, New York City is four hours ahead of Los Angeles and six hours ahead of Honolulu! Sometimes, a few hours can make the difference.

America's Busiest Airports

Air travel is no longer for the privileged and few. Flying from one place to another is commonplace and has opened travel opportunities to all people as is reflected by the record number of people who fly these days. Listed below are the 10 busiest airports in terms of passengers who arrived or departed.[2]

1.	Chicago/O'Hare	67,254,586
2.	Atlanta	57,734,755
3.	Dallas/Ft. Worth	54,298,930
4.	Los Angeles	53,909,223
5.	San Francisco	36,260,064
6.	Miami	33,235,658
7.	Denver	31,028,191
8.	New York/JFK	30,327,723
9.	Detroit	29,013,260
10.	Las Vegas	28,001,258

PROMOTIONS AND DISCOUNT COUPONS. You wouldn't believe me if I told you how many discount coupon offers and promotions hit the market each and every day. Don't assume these are *only* applicable to vacation travel. I've see offers and discount coupons that save business travelers a fortune!

Most discount coupon and certificate programs offer:
- Free tickets
- Reduced-rate tickets
- Buy one, get one free or Companion tickets
- Special, unpublished fares
- Savings, usually $25-$100, off the fare
- Upgrades

Where do I find these coupons and deals? Everywhere. They really are everywhere. In your grocery store, credit card statements, place of employment, magazines, junk mail, discount coupon books, travel clubs, and many retail stores.

Where is the last place I'll probably find them? Travel agencies. Sorry guys, but it's true! Travel agencies are not operationally geared to hustle discount coupons and other promotional offers. It's just the nature of the beast! Most travel agencies are dependant upon the airlines, cruise lines, hotels, and car rental companies for their discount information. Travel suppliers rarely advise travel agents of discounts and promotions that are put out directly to the public. Unfortunately, many consumers are not aware of these offers either.

An aggressive travel agent can be a good source of discount travel, especially fare wars and some promotions. But hundreds of free and discounted travel offers are distributed outside the travel agency network. Travel agents are simply not equipped to be a resource of discount coupons. *How many of the offers listed in Chapter One did you hear about from your travel agent?*

Don't misunderstand me about travel agencies. A good travel agent can be a great help. Travel agents are probably the most overworked and underpaid group in America. I have always recommended the use of a good travel agency or travel club. The truth of the matter is that travel agencies, which are paid commissions by the travel suppliers on their sales, cannot afford to be discount coupon brokers.

There are no mandatory professional standards to be a travel agent. If I, as a travel agency owner and manager, hire you, you become a travel agent. No training or professional competency level is required. Most travel agencies provide in-house operational and destination training. Most travel agents take their work seriously and seek out the best fare for you, but simply are not on top of the hundreds of discount coupons and promotional coupons that hit the market.

If I were to choose a travel agent, this is what I would consider:

- **Personal recommendations.** Ask friends who they have used and if they've been pleased.
- Is the travel agency a member of any professional organizations, such as **ASTA** (American Society of Travel Agents), **ARTA** (Association of Retail Travel Agents), and/or **CLIA** (Cruise Lines International Association)? This is no guarantee of competency, but helps you to know that an agency takes their business seriously enough to join professional ranks.
- Does the travel agent have a **CTC** designation (Certified Travel Consultant)? This professional designation requires considerable time, work, and committment.
- Have any agents been professionally designated as a **"specialist?"** Not just being named a specialist by the agency manager, but having received the designation from a recognized industry group or organization. For example, the Australian Tourist Commission will designate selected agents as "Aussie Specialists" who are proven and certified to be experts in travel to Australia. Specialist agents are a gold mine of information!
- What **personal experience** does the agent have with destinations, tours, cruises, airlines, and other travel suppliers? No agent can be

an expert in everything. That's why you are looking for a specialist or an experienced, knowledgable agent.

- Does the agency have a good **resource library** and materials?
- Does the agent **go beyond the "first answer or response"** given by the computer or other sources? No computer can replace the creative mind!
- This may be the most important. **Is the travel agent creative?** Does he or she constantly give you options and suggest ways of saving money? Or is the agent more of an "order taker?" Is the agent aware of the "tricks of the trade?"
- Here's a biggie to me. **Do you feel that you are important** to your travel agent? Does your agent take a personal interest in you? Are you treated like a friend, or just part of the herd?

Here is a good test of creativity and street smarts: Go back to Chapter One which listed travel bargains that are or have been recently available. Remember, this list is only a sampling, the tip of the iceberg. Now, ask yourself this question, "How many of these deals did my travel agent tell me about?" "Did I know about any of them?" If so, "What was my source?" (If you listen to the *Travel Show* you knew about every one of these and many, many more!)

Bottom line, you must find a travel information source that is constantly giving you tips, recommendations, and insider secrets to killer travel deals! What you don't know can hurt you!

OK, so what do I do? Find an information source. You need a "street smart" guy or company to hustle for you. Is your "street smart" guy creative? Does he/she offer options? Does he/she always try to ethically and legally beat the system and the price?

Where did you find your guy? The best sources are legitimate travel clubs,[3] travel programs like the *Travel Show*, travel newsletters and magazines that focus on discount promotions, and discount minded travel agencies.

Can you find out about these deals on your own? Yes. However, your ability to do so may be limited by time, experience, and resources.

CONSOLIDATORS. Memorize this word. It will save you a bundle. Airlines can project with a high degree of accuracy the "load factor" (percentage of seats occupied) on any given flight. Airline inventory is unlike most merchandise in that it is time sensitive. If I own an auto parts store and only sell five of my 20 spark plugs on Monday, I can hold onto the remaining 15 and hope to sell them Tuesday or Wednesday. Or, if I am selling bananas and the unsold fruit starts to turn brown, I can change directions and make banana nut bread. An unsold airline seat is a perishable commodity. Once the plane door closes, the seat goes empty, stays empty, and arrives empty. Translation: Lost revenue for the airline. So what do the carriers do? They find *alternative distribution* channels (translation: lower prices). "Alternative distribution" is a fancy term for finding someone to sell airline tickets to without upsetting normal sales distribution channels (translation: higher prices). You will not get a **consolidator fare** from the airline. Most travel agencies do not have their own consolidator contracts, but rely on third parties or **consolidators**, from which they buy their discounted tickets.

There is no fixed or set price for a consolidator ticket. In most cases, an airline will give a consolidator (also known as a "ticket consolidator" and referred to in Europe as a "bucket shop") a net rate, which the consolidator, in turn, marks up and sells either to travel agencies, the public, or both. The fare may even be open to negotiation between you and your travel agent.

Consolidator fares to Europe usually discount the lowest published fares 10-20 percent. Fares to Asia may drop anywhere from 20-50 percent below the lowest published fares. Consolidator tickets are available to most areas of the world. The discounts will differ from consolidator to consolidator and by local market conditions.

Consolidator tickets are usually restrictive tickets, but may waive some ticketing requirements, such as advance purchase, minimum/maximum stay. Typical restrictions may include limitations on itinerary changes. Know all the terms, conditions, and restrictions before you buy.

Some consolidators sell to the general public, others work exclusively with travel agents. An excellent resource guide to consolidator tickets is *The Index To Air Travel Consolidators*, by Gary Schmidt, Travel Publishing, Inc. Telephone 800-241-9299 or 612-292-0325. The book lists all major consolidators and notes the destinations and airlines each company works with. It also informs you which consolidators work with the public and which do not.

A word of caution. Be careful who you deal with. I read of travel agency and consolidator failures all the time. If they sink, your money sinks with them. Recommendations and past experience is the best advice. The Sunday travel section of the *New York Times, Los Angeles Times,* or other major newspapers from either coast, are excellent sources of current consolidators and consolidator fares. Pay only with a credit card, which may give you some measure of protection and refund in the event of a travel agency or consolidator failure.

Work with a travel agency or travel club when buying a consolidator ticket. Unfortunately, I know of travelers who have been stranded because the airline involved in their consolidator ticket did not honor the ticket, usually because the consolidator had violated some provision of their airline agreement. Sometimes a consolidator has been known to accept a client's money, but the consolidator does not pay the airline for the ticket. The airline then demands payment from the passenger. If you encounter a problem with your ticket, you may have recourse with your travel agent.

Listed below are consolidators that sell to the general public. Compare your price buying direct from a consolidator with your travel agency or travel club price. Some consolidators will sell a ticket at the same price to both the public and to travel agencies. Most consolidators, however, will discount the price to travel agencies. Some consolidators sell only to travel agencies. Your travel agency or travel club may provide you an additional discount. If the consolidator direct price to you is the same or similar to the consolidator travel agency price, always use a travel agency. Not only will you receive more services, but if you run into any problems, it will be much easier to resolve the problems with a travel agency rather than with a consolidator.

Amirang Travel	800-223-6225	Asia
Columbus Travel	800-373-3328	South Pacific
D-FW Tours	800-527-2589	Europe, Middle East, Orient, Africa
DER Travel Service	800-717-4247	Europe, Middle East, Africa
East-West Tours	800-435-9247	Eastern Europe
Express Discount	800-266-8669	Mexico
General Tours	800-221-2261	Europe, Middle East, Africa, India.
Fantasy Holidays	800-645-2555	Europe
Magical Holidays	800-228-2208	Europe, Middle East, Africa, Latin America
Premier Travel	800-435-9247	South Africa
Unitravel	800-325-2222	Europe, Orient, Africa, Latin America

ALTERNATE CITIES. I received a call from Sara, a listener in Salt Lake City who had planned a trip to Washington, D.C. Of course, she wanted the lowest possible price. The lowest fare to Washington, D.C. at this time was $298. I suggested she fly into Baltimore where the round-trip fare was only $154. Sara said she was planning to rent a car, so the extra 25 miles driving from Baltimore to downtown D.C. didn't make any difference. She saved $144 because she flew to an alternate city.

Did we stop there? No! (I told you this is a challenging game to me!) I told Sara of an American Airlines promotion coupon that would reduce her fare by $25. Now she is only paying $129 round-trip compared to $298. Are we done? No way. I suggested a special hotel rate of $89 available through a hotel consolidator instead of the regular rate of $195. Done now? Nope! I told her of a special Alamo Rent A Car rate which dropped her car rental an additional 15 percent and gave her a free upgrade to a larger car. She also received frequent flyer miles on her airline ticket, hotel, and car rental from each travel supplier. She earned miles for using her airline affinity credit card.

It is a good idea to always check the fares to alternate or nearby cities. You may save hundreds of dollars in the process. There are many alternative city pairs. A list is provided in this chapter.

Here are alternate city round-trip fare examples:[4]

Sarasota/Seattle	Lowest fare:	$458
Tampa/Seattle	Lowest fare:	$358
	Savings:	$100
San Jose/Atlanta	Lowest fare:	$376
San Francisco/Atlanta	Lowest fare:	$299
	Savings:	$ 77
Phoenix/Washington, D.C.	Lowest fare:	$460
Phoenix/Baltimore	Lowest fare:	$192
	Savings:	$268

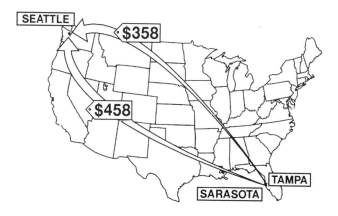

Recently I took a call on the *Travel Show* from Scott in Amarillo, Texas. Scott, his wife, and four children were planning a trip to Washington, D.C. On the day of the call, the lowest published round-trip fare from Amarillo to Washington, D.C. was $383. How could we reduce their travel cost if $383 was absolutely, positively, the rock bottom fare?

First, I told him of a discount book available for sale in his area. The cost of the book was about $20 and included several discount airline coupons valid for travel on American Airlines or Continental Airlines. (The American coupon was also being accepted by Northwest Airlines.) Use of the coupons would reduce *each* ticket by $75. Now his round-trip fare, with the $75 discount, was only $308 per person. That's a family savings of $450!

I also suggested that he consider an alternate city; Albuquerque is only a three or four hour drive from Amarillo. USAir was offering a special $178 round-trip fare from Albuquerque to Washington, D.C. This would provide a $205 per person savings ($1,230 for the family) off the original $383 fare. A $130 per person savings off the coupon discounted fare of $308 ($780 for the family) if he purchased the coupon book I told him about. I asked him, "Is it worth $780 or $1,230 for your family to drive to Albuquerque?" Scott thought that was an easy question to answer! (More about discount airline coupons later.)

There are hundreds of alternate city pairs. It's a good idea to become somewhat familiar with nearby cities as they may offer a substantial fare savings. Better yet, your agent should be offering alternatives. If not, find a new agent! You can't afford your present one!

Alternate Cities

When looking for the best fare, always check alternate cities that are close to your destination. Sometimes you can save a significant amount of money by flying to a nearby city. All alternate cities listed below are within 100 air miles of the destination city. If you are planning to rent a car anyway, your transportation costs to your destination city are already taken care of.

Destination City	Alternate Cities
Akron, OH	Cleveland, Pittsburgh, Columbus
Albany, NY	Hartford
Atlanta, GA	Chattanooga
Atlantic City, NJ	Philadelphia, Newark, New York City
Austin, TX	San Antonio, Houston
Baltimore, MD	Washington, D.C., Philadelphia
Baton Rouge, LA	New Orleans
Boston, MA	Providence, Hartford
Buffalo, NY	Rochester
Burbank, CA	Los Angeles, Ontario, Orange County
Burlington, VT	Montreal
Charleston, SC	Columbia
Charlotte, NC	Greensboro

Chattanooga, TN	Knoxville
Chicago, IL	Milwaukee
Cincinnati, OH	Dayton, Louisville, Indianapolis
Colorado Springs, CO	Denver
Columbus, OH	Dayton
Dayton, OH	Cincinnati, Columbus
Daytona Beach, FL	Orlando, Jacksonville
Denver, CO	Colorado Springs
Detroit, MI	Toledo, Lansing
Evansville, IN	Louisville
Flint, MI	Lansing, Detroit
Fort Lauderdale, FL	Miami, West Palm Beach
Grand Rapids, MI	Lansing
Greensboro, NC	Raleigh, Charlotte
Harrisburg, PA	Baltimore, Philadelphia, Washington, D.C.
Hartford, CT	Boston
Hilton Head, SC	Savannah
Huntsville, AL	Birmingham
Indianapolis, IN	Cincinnati
Kalamazoo, MI	Lansing
Lansing, MI	Grand Rapids, Detroit
Lexington, KY	Louisville, Cincinnati
Lincoln, NE	Omaha
Los Angeles, CA	Burbank, Ontario, Orange County
Louisville, KY	Cincinnati
Madison, WI	Milwaukee
Manchester, MA	Boston
McAllen, TX	Harlingen
Miami, FL	Fort Lauderdale, West Palm Beach
Milwaukee, WI	Chicago
Mobile, AL	Pensacola
Montreal, Canada	Burlington
Naples, FL	Fort Myers
New Orleans, LA	Baton Rouge
New York City, NY	Newark, Philadelphia
Newark, NJ	New York City, Philadelphia
Norfolk, VA	Newport News, Richmond
Oakland, CA	San Francisco, San Jose, Sacramento
Ontario, CA	Burbank, Los Angeles, Orange County
Orange County, CA	Burbank, Los Angeles, Ontario, San Diego

Orlando, FL	Tampa
Palm Springs, CA	Ontario, San Diego
Philadelphia, PA	Newark, Baltimore, Harrisburg, New York City
Portland, ME	Boston
Providence, RI	Boston, Hartford
Raleigh, NC	Greensboro
Richmond, VA	Newport News; Washington, D.C.
Roanoke, VA	Greensboro
Rochester, NY	Buffalo, Syracuse
Sacramento, CA	Oakland, San Francisco
Saginaw, MI	Lansing, Detroit
San Diego, CA	Orange County
San Francisco, CA	Oakland, San Jose, Sacramento
San Jose, CA	San Francisco, Oakland
Sarasota, FL	Tampa
South Bend, IN	Chicago
St. George, UT	Las Vegas, Cedar City
Syracuse, NY	Rochester
Tampa, FL	Orlando
Toledo, OH	Detroit
Washington, D.C.	Baltimore, Richmond
West Palm Beach, FL	Fort Lauderdale, Miami
Worchester, MA	Providence, Boston, Hartford

BACK-TO-BACK TICKETING. Do you really want to see an OUCH fare? Look at the difference between unrestricted fares ("Y" Coach Class) and discount restricted fares, which may require a Saturday night stay and other restrictions. The airlines have their collective "sights" on the business travel.

Tom needs to fly from Dallas to Washington, D.C. on Monday, October 7, and return home on Thursday, October 10. Here are the lowest available, unrestricted and restricted fares at the time of booking. The less expensive restrictive fare requires a "Saturday-night stay," the more expensive, unrestricted fare does not.

How can Tom save some money? Okay, let's take a stab at it.

Routing: Dallas/ Washington, D.C. round-trip.

Unrestricted "Y" Class Coach ticket: $ 647 each way, or
                                                             $1,294 round-trip

Restricted ticket with Saturday-night stay: $ 262 round-trip

Okay, Tom has two options:

Option 1: Buy a round-trip "Y" class (full fare) ticket for $ 1,294. He doesn't "qualify" for the restricted, Saturday-night stay ticket since he is returning home on Thursday.

Option 2: Buy two (yes, you heard me say two) round-trip restricted Saturday-night stay tickets. Here's how it works:

Ticket 1:
This Monday, October 7: Dallas to Washington, D.C.   **Segment 1**
Next Thursday, October 17: Washington, D.C. to Dallas Segment 2

Ticket 2:
This Thursday, October 10: Washington, D.C. to Dallas **Segment 3**
Next Monday, October 14: Dallas to Washington, D.C.   Segment 4

The combined price of the two less expensive, restricted tickets is $524 compared to the normal unrestrictive fare of $1,294 that other business travelers are paying. For his "real" trip, Tom uses ticket 1, segment 1 for October 7, and ticket 2, segment 3 for October 10. Tom could either throw the unused tickets away, or make another trip if he knows his travel dates. If he takes a second trip to Washington, D.C., he uses segments 2 and 4, provided he travels on the ticketed dates. Even if Tom doesn't return to Washington, D.C. on his "throw away" tickets, by purchasing two lower priced tickets, he saved $770.

Tom could also consider an alternate city fare. His unrestricted round-trip fare of $1,294 to Washington, D.C. is reduced to $910 round-trip ($455 each way and unrestricted) if he were to fly in and out of Baltimore.

Here's another savings angle. Many airlines offer special weekend fares that require a Saturday departure and a return the following Monday or Tuesday. The "weekend" fare from Dallas to Washington, D.C. is only $178 round-trip. Two weekend round-trip tickets cost Tom only $356.

Caution. Remember that restrictive tickets are just that! Restrictive and usually non-refundable. Itinerary changes, if allowed, are an additional fee. This practice, known as "back-to-back" ticketing, is legal, although some airlines insist the practice violates *their* rules. *Their* rules are not to be confused with federal or state statute. Other airlines have announced they simply don't care and just want the passenger on their plane. Some travelers use different airlines for ticket 1 and ticket 2. Most promotional or discount fares require an advance purchase. Business and last minute travelers may not always have the convenience of knowing when they must travel.

Remember, combine these savings with promotional discounts that can reduce your fare to record lows!

BREAKING THE FARE. Few things in life are as much fun as reducing the cost of travel and finding new ways to drop the bottom out of airfares. Breaking Fares? Yep! Also known as "split ticketing."

You remember that a "through fare" is the cost of a ticket from City A to City B. Breaking the fare refers to a creative (and legal) ticketing strategy that can save hundreds of dollars. Here is an example:

Mark, from Salt Lake City, called the *Travel Show* and wanted the lowest fare (don't they all?) to Anchorage for him and his wife. The lowest round-trip fare was $442 on Delta. Actually, that was a pretty good fare because the "through" fares had been over $700. What could I do, he asked?

I saved Mark and his wife $258. Here's what I suggested. Two people can fly from Salt Lake City to Seattle using a round-trip "companion fare" for only $109 each.[5] From Seattle to Anchorage, the per person round-trip fare was $204. The combined fare was reduced to only $313 and a savings of $129 each, or $258 for the two. That's *Shop Smart!*

I love saving people money! Jennifer called me from Denver. She wanted to fly to Fort Lauderdale and wanted to save some money. (Am I seeing a pattern here?) She told me the lowest round-trip fare she could find was $452. She had called three travel agencies and two airlines and they all quoted her the same $452 fare. What she had been told was technically correct. The lowest published round-trip fare from Denver to Fort Lauderdale was $452.

Here was my suggestion. Why not "break the fare?" There is no non-stop service between Denver and Fort Lauderdale.[6] Jennifer will have to make a connection and change planes somewhere. Why not in Kansas City? She could fly from Denver to Kansas City for $142. Her fare from

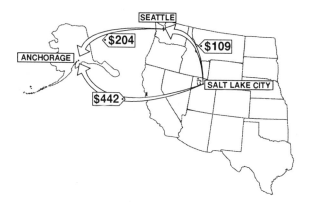

Kansas City to Fort Lauderdale was $198. Her round-trip fare total was only $340, saving her $112.

Got time for one more? Mike from Portland called the ***Travel Show*** and he's taking the family to Orlando. Dad, Mom, and two kids. He didn't buy any tickets during a fare war (shame on him!) and was sweating the high fares. Mike's in a tough jam. He promised the family they would go and they had even picked the date. There was no backing out of this one!

The best fare from Portland to Orlando was $476 round-trip. Here's how we saved his trip and his wallet. You got it! Break the fare. There is no non-stop service between Portland and Orlando, so where shall we change planes? Well, how does Salt Lake City grab ya? It grabbed Mike just fine!

I suggested Mike fly from Portland to Salt Lake City using a Delta companion fare for only $109 per person. From there, change planes and fly non-stop on Delta (good connection, Delta to Delta) for only $238. Total fare: $347 each. Total savings: $129 per person and $516 for the family.

Breaking the fare not only works on round-trip fares, but can often help the one-way traveler. Ken was planning to fly one-way from Dallas to Chicago. The lowest one-way fare was $421. I suggested an alternative that doesn't appear in the CRS of any travel agent or airline.

Ken could fly from Dallas to Kansas City on American for $59, and from Kansas City to Chicago also on American for $44. His one-way fare is now only $103 and he saved $319. It is most convenient to fly non-stop. Is it worth an additional $319? I'll let you answer that one!

Can you always reduce your ticket cost by "breaking the fare?" No. Sometimes issuing two tickets rather than one "through fare" can actually result in a higher fare. The issue is creative ticketing. One should be obsessed with finding ways to reduce travel costs! Breaking fares is just one of those ways that ***Shop Smart*** travelers look at.

POINT BEYOND FARES. You want to travel from City A to City B and the fare is $300. You also know that your plane flies from City A to City B and then on to City C. The fare from City A to City C is only $250. So what do you do? Buy a ticket to City C and then just get off in City B and save $50. This is called a "Point Beyond Fare" or a "Hidden-City Fare."

For example, the lowest fare from St. Louis to Washington, D.C. is $449 round-trip. The lowest fare from Kansas City to the capital on TWA is $198 round-trip. All TWA flights from Kansas City to Washington, D.C. stop in and require a change of planes in St. Louis. One could buy an "open jaw" round-trip ticket from St. Louis to Washington, D.C. on the outbound (going portion), and from Washington, D.C. to Kansas City on the return (with a stop in St. Louis) for only $323.50. This fare is calculated by using half of the St. Louis/Washington, D.C. fare and half of the Washington, D.C./Kansas City fare. The passenger simply gets off the plane in St. Louis on his return leg and pockets the savings of $125.50.

Or, suppose you need to fly one-way from Washington, D.C. to St. Louis and do not have enough time to buy the ticket in advance so as to obtain a lower priced restricted ticket. The lowest one-way fare from Washington, D.C. to Kansas City on TWA is $399. The lowest one-way ticket from the capital to St. Louis with no advance purchase is $500. You buy a ticket to Kansas City, knowing that your plane stops in St. Louis. You get off the plane in St. Louis and not take the final leg to Kansas City and save $101.

Cautions: It sounds easy, but here are some red flags:
- Your luggage can only be checked to your *final* destination. So just take carry-on bags.
- If you "no show" for a flight, your onward (or future) reservation segments will be canceled. If you use a "Point Beyond Fare" on a round-trip ticket, use it on the return.
- Airlines take a dim view of this practice and allege that it violates their ticket rules, i.e., the terms and conditions of carriage.
- If you choose to use "Point Beyond Fares," don't broadcast your intent. Airlines consider it improper and most travel agents are fearful that the airline will beat 'em up for knowingly issuing such a ticket. Just tell your agent what tickets you want without explaining why. I do not necessarily endorse this practice, but include it here because I am constantly asked about it.
- The easiest use of "Point Beyond Fares" are one-way tickets or on the return portion of a round-trip ticket.

With regards to the legal question of so-called "Point Beyond Fares" or "Hidden-City Fares," the issue may soon be settled in court. "Two lawsuits on hidden-city ticketing are in the works. The first, seeking $500 million on behalf of travelers, results from Northwest Airlines nabbing a passenger at the airport and charging him the full fare. The passenger turned out to be a lawyer. The second suit will be filed on behalf of travel agents, some of whom have been hit by airlines with debit memos amounting to tens of thousands of dollars."[7]

BUY A LOWER PRICED ROUND-TRIP TICKET, *even when you only need a one-way ticket.* This is the easiest form of saving big dollars on one-way travel. One-way travel, usually an unrestricted ticket, is often outrageously priced. In many cases, it is less expensive to buy a round-trip ticket, use just the outbound or going portion of the ticket, and throw away the return portion. Always check one-way fares. In some markets there are low one-way prices.

I remember a listener in Boston called the *Travel Show* and explained she needed to fly to Los Angeles where she would pick-up her father's car and drive it back home to Boston. She had been quoted $534 for a one-way ticket. I suggested she buy a discounted round-trip fare of only $280, use the Boston to Los Angeles portion, discard the return and pocket the savings! That's how to *Shop Smart!*

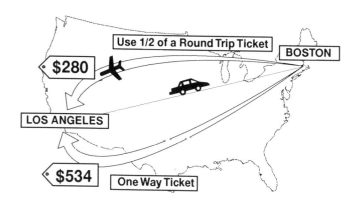

INTERNATIONAL AIRLINE PASSES. International airline passes can significantly reduce your cost on overseas flights. These are not trans-oceanic flights, but are regional passes. Contact the airlines named with each pass for current fares and routings.
Africa.
•   South African Airways offers the *African Explorer* pass with four to eight flights to be taken within a 30-day period.

Asia.

- Garuda offers the *Visit Indonesia Air Pass* with various options on the length and number of flights allowed.
- Malaysia Airlines sells a *Discover Malaysia* pass which allows five flights within 21 days.
- Silk Air, in conjunction with Singapore Airlines, offers a regional air pass.
- Thai Air offers a *National Heritage Pass* good for four flights within 60 days.

Caribbean.

- Bahamasair offers the *AirPass* which includes Miami and the out islands of the Bahamas valid for three flights within 21 days.
- Liat offers both the *Caribbean Explorer Pass* good for three flights within 21 days to your choice of three islands and the *Super Caribbean Explorer Pass* which is valid to any island within 30 days.

India.

- Indian Air Lines offers a *Discover India Pass* for 21 days of unlimited travel. The India *Wonderfare* offers seven days of unlimited travel within four regions.

Europe.

- Air France, Air Inter, Sabena, and Czechoslovak Airlines offer *Euroflyer* passes. Travel must originate in Paris, Brussels, or Prague and is valid to about 100 European cities over a stay of seven days to two months.
- Air France offers *La France Pass* good for seven days of travel within France to be taken during a 30-day period.
- British Airways, Deutsche BA, and TAT European Airlines offer a pass of three to twelve legs for travel throughout Eastern and Western Europe.
- Lufthansa, Finnair, Lauda Air, and United Airlines offer a pass program based upon flight segments within Europe.
- Swissair, Austrian Airlines, Cross Air, and Tyrolean Airways offer a visitors pass for flights originating in Austria or Switzerland for travel throughout Europe.
- Finnair offers the *Holiday Ticket* with 10 segments valid for 30 days within Finland.
- Alitalia offers the *Visit Italy Pass* good for three, four, or six segments good for 90 days.

- SAS sells a *Visit Scandinavia Pass* for three, four, or six segments good for 90 days.

South America.

- Aerolineas Argentinas sells a four to eight segment pass.
- Varig's *Visit Brazil Pass* is one of the most popular airline passes. You can visit up to five cities within a 21-day period.
- Lloyd Aero Boliviano offers the *Visit Bolivia Pass* good for travel up to six cities in Bolivia within a 28-day period.
- Lan Chile offers the *Visit Chile Fare* good for travel to nine cities within 21 days.
- Avianca sells the *Discover Columbia Pass* valid for ten flights within 30 days.
- Aeroperu offers a program for travel within Peru and a program covering all of South America. Another Aeroperu pass program is for intra-Peru flights only.
- Avensa Airlines offers the *Avensa Airpass* for 45 days of travel within Venezuela.

South Pacific.

- Air Pacific offers the *Pacific Air Pass*. Various destinations and prices are available.
- Air Nuigini sells a four flight pass.
- Fiji Air offers a four segment *Discover Fiji Pass*. Travel within 30 days.
- Polynesian Airlines offers the *Pacific Explorer Pass* good for travel to Samoa, Tonga, Fiji, Cook Islands, New Zealand, and Australia.
- Qantas and Air New Zealand participate in *Down Under Discount Deals*. Prices are determined by cities selected.

Insider Tip: Always keep a photo copy of your passport information pages with you. The information pages contain your photograph and personal information, including your passport number. Keep the photo copy separate from your passport. In the unlikely event you lose your passport overseas, submitting a photo copy to the nearest United States Embassy or Consulate General will expedite your passport replacement process.

SPECIAL CIRCUMSTANCE TRAVEL. Airlines may offer discounts for special circumstance travel, including senior citizens, children, military personnel, group travel, student and youth fares, compassion and bereavement fares for family emergencies, family discounts, foreign visitor

Watch Your Tags

I make it a habit to always look over my luggage claim tags after I have checked in a bag. Claim checks will have the three letter airport code of your final destination written on them.

Not long ago, I was returning from Frankfurt (FRA), Germany, to Salt Lake City (SLC). As I was was walking away from the airline check-in counter, I noticed that my bags were being sent to SCL rather than SLC. This is no small mistake. SCL is Santiago, Chile! As in South America. As in adiós to my luggage! SLC is Salt Lake City. As in Utah. As in U.S.A.!

I returned to the counter and notified the agent of the error. She profusely apologized, retreived my luggage and properly tagged them. Imagine the embarassment for an efficient German!

passes and discounts, and so on. I think you get the picture.

The best source of information on special circumstance discounts is your professional travel agent. Here are just a few highlights.

Senior Citizen. Depending on who you talk to, a "senior citizen" is anyone 50, 55, 60, 62, or 65 years or older. There is a wealth of discounts available if you ask for them. It never hurts to ask, the worst case is you are told "no" and then are just back where you began.

Most U.S. airlines usually define a senior citizen as anyone over 62, except on Southwest, age 65. Each airline has their own definition. With most fares, you receive a 10 percent discount. This discount may also be applicable to your traveling companion of any age. Read chapter eight for details on senior citizen discounts.

Compassion and Bereavement Fares. Many airlines will offer a discount to individuals traveling due to some family emergency, death, or illness. Unfortunately, these fares usually offer a savings off the unrestricted full fare and not a discount off the lower, restricted fare levels. Discounts typically run 30 to 40 percent. You may be required to show proof of your family emergency, such as a death certificate.

CHILDREN. Always ask for children's discounts. Most domestic fares have one price, regardless of age, but it never hurts to ask. There are still children's fares in some markets.

I see a lot of children's promotions. Delta Air Lines offers one of the best.

Delta Air Lines' Fantastic Flyer Program. Children ages two through 12 can be enrolled in this program and receive discount travel coupons. Once enrolled, you will receive a membership kit that includes a free subscription to *Fantastic Flyer* magazine and other goodies for the kids. Here's what *you* are looking for in the kit: a coupon good for a 20 percent

The World's Best Airlines

Readers of *Travel and Leisure*[8] and *Condé Nast Traveler*[9] magazines rated the airlines. The first category includes all airlines flying international routes. The second category was for U.S. carriers flying their domestic routes.

World's Best International Airlines

Travel and Leisure	Condé Nast Traveler
1. Singapore Airlines	1. Singapore Airlines
2. Swissair	2. Swissair
3. Cathay Pacific	3. Virgin Atlantic
4. Qantas	4. Qantas
5. Thai International	5. British Airways
6. Air New Zealand	6. SAS
7. Japan Airlines	7. KLM Royal Dutch Airlines
8. British Airways	8. Air New Zealand
9. Virgin Atlantic	9. Cathay Pacific
10. Lufthansa	10. Lufthansa

It is interesting to note that U.S. carriers flying international routes were included in both surveys, but none finished in the top 10. The *Travel and Leisure* survey only rank ordered 10 airlines. *Condé Nast Traveler* ranked their top 20 airlines. In this survey, the top U.S. international airlines were Alaska Airlines at #14; United Airlines at #16; and Delta Air Lines at #19.

Top U.S. Domestic Airlines

Travel and Leisure	Condé Nast Traveler
1. Alaska Airlines	1. Midwest Express Airlines
2. United Airlines	2. Alaska Airlines
3. Delta Air Lines	3. United Airlines
4. American Airlines	4. Delta Air Lines
5. Hawaiian Airlines	5. American Airlines
6. Northwest Airlines	6. Kiwi International
7. Aloha Airlines	7. Southwest Airlines
8. TWA	8. Hawaiian Airlines
9. America West Airlines	9. TWA
10. Southwest Airlines	10. Northwest Airlines

discount that covers your child and up to three family members traveling together. Now pay attention. The coupon is good for 120 days after enrollment. If you are planning a trip more than four months from now, wait to enroll your child until you can fall within the four month validity. The 20 percent discount is applicable to fares of $198 or more. There are some holiday blackout dates. How do you enroll? Call Delta at 800-392-KIDS (5437), or enroll online at *http:www.delta-air.com/fantastic.*

Kids Fly Free. One of the more common travel promotions for children is a "kids fly free" offer. There doesn't seem to be any hard and fast pattern, but every year I see several. Watch your local papers, look in parenting magazines, and ask your travel club or travel agent to advise you when one hits the market. Be prepared to act fast because these free seats go fast!

Special Promotions. There is a constant flood of special discount programs for children traveling with adults. Almost every magazine that deals with families and children will include a special promotional offer at some point. For example, not long ago *Parents* magazine included a $129 companion fare certificate. Nothing extra to buy. Nothing to fill out. Just detach the coupon from the magazine and buy your ticket.

International Travel: While children's discounts have largely, but not completely, disappeared for domestic travel (except for special one-time promotions), many international routes still offer good discounts for children ages two through 11. A 12-year old is considered an adult. Typically, the children's fare on international tickets is two-thirds, sometimes even half, of the adult fare. Most international airlines charge a 10 percent fee for infants being held, even though the infant does not get a seat.

STUDENT AND YOUTH FARES. Most student and youth travel is considered discretionary by the airlines and therefore subject to various discount offers. Most so-called "student standby fares" are a thing of the past. Airlines quickly discovered that students would call using phony names and make multiple reservations so that a flight would appear full, but then have dozens of "no shows" which would allow students waiting as "stand-by fares" to travel at drastically reduced, last-minute fares.

Many airlines will offer a special student fare for both domestic and international travel. Often the fare does not allow a lot of advance planning. TWA's youth fares allow no more than a three-day advance reservation. Here are some pretty good youth programs:

TWA Youth Travel Pak. Students between the ages of 14 and 24 are eligible to purchase a $548 book of four domestic flight coupons. Each coupon is good for a one-way trip; two coupons required for round-trip travel. A 20 percent discount on European travel is also included. Here's one of the best features — there are no blackout dates, although travel is not permitted between 12 noon and 7:00 p.m. on Sundays. Students may travel during the holiday periods at low ball prices. To order, call your travel agent or TWA at 800-221-2000.

Travel U. MasterCard's AT&T Universal Card offers the Travel U program that includes three USAir discount certificates. Additional certificates are automatically issued every six months. Discount fares include both domestic and international travel and can reduce ticket prices up to 46 percent. For information, call 800-438-8627

Student Privileges. American Express and Continental Airlines have teamed up to offer discount fares to full-time college students who have a Student Privileges American Express Card. Upon enrollment, you receive five discount certificates valid on Continental Airlines. The program entitles you to purchase a discounted companion fare at the same price and with no age restrictions. You will also receive an MCI calling card good for 30 minutes of long-distance calling each month, and a 15 percent discount off Amtrak fares. Call American Express at 800-582-5823 to enroll.

Student Getaway. TWA offers the Student Getaway program open to full-time high school and college students ages 16 to 26. The program will give students a 10 percent discount off most domestic and international fares. A one year membership card costs $15. A two year card costs $25. Call your travel agent or TWA at 800-221-2000.

America West. This airline offers a 10 percent discount to students ages 15-17 on flights to Mexico. You may be required to show proof of age and student enrollment. For more information, contact your travel agent or America West at 800-235-9292.

Where To Complain?

Do you have a complaint regarding an airline? Baggage handling, refunds, advertising, or customer service? If so, go first to the airline and attempt to resolve the problem. You can get their number by calling the reservation department of the airline you're beefed at and ask them for the number of the Customer Service or Consumer Affairs Department. State your complaint clearly and work with the airline to resolve your dispute.

If that fails, you can make a formal complaint to the feds.

Airline service and injury complaints:
Aviation Consumer Protection Division
U.S. Department of Transportation, C-75
400 - 7th Street S.W., Room 4107
Washington, D.C. 20590
Telephone 202-366-2220

Airline safety issues:
Federal Aviation Administration
800 Independence Ave., S.W.
Washington, D.C. 20591
Telephone 800-322-7873

CREDIT CARDS AND FREQUENT FLYER AWARDS. How much do you spend each year? Total expenditures? Use an airline affinity credit card and earn airline frequent flyer miles that can be redeemed for FREE air tickets, cruises, car rentals, hotel and resort stays, tours, and merchandise.

Here's how it works. Some credit cards offer one or more airline frequent flyer miles for every dollar you spend. Is the mileage credit only for travel purchases? No. With an airline affinity credit card, you receive frequent flyer points for all credit card purchases. Most people get nothing for their charges. Why not earn free miles and free tickets?

Airline affinity credit cards offer a mileage program with one airline. The American Express Membership Miles allows you to designate which participating airline you want all or part of your miles to go to. Your mileage credit remains in a "bank account" until you withdraw the needed miles for a free trip. The remaining balance is yours to use whenever you choose.

Want to know which ones gives you mileage on your preferred airline? Easy! Ask that airline. You can also ask your travel agent to provide you with a list of affinity credit cards and their participating airlines. I suggest you concentrate your miles on one or two airlines. Your awards will accrue faster than trying to spread your miles over many carriers. Here are some airline affinity credit cards:

Alaska Airlines VISA or MasterCard	800-442-6680
America West VISA or MasterCard	800-508-2933
American AAdvantage VISA or MasterCard	800-359-4444
Continental OnePass VISA or MasterCard	800-850-3144
Delta SkyMiles American Express	800-759-6453
Midwest Express MasterCard	800-388-4044
Northwest WorldPerks VISA	800-360-2900
Southwest Rapid Rewards VISA	800-792-8472
TWA VISA or MasterCard	800-632-5080
United Mileage Plus VISA or MasterCard	800-537-7783
USAir VISA	800-294-0849

Here's an interesting scenario for earning air miles fast and **Shop Smart**. Suppose you use an airline affinity credit card for almost everything you purchase.[10] Let's see what you can earn.

<u>**Expense Item:**</u>	<u>**Miles Earned:**</u>
Dining out. Assume you spend $50 a week on personal dining out and $110 monthly on business meals. Total: $3,720. You can earn 10 miles per dollar spent with a Diners Club card. Delta Sky Miles will award three miles for every dollar spent at participating restaurants. For our example, assume only $1,000 is spent at such restaurants.	**40,200**
Charge everything. Sign up for an airline affinity card and get 10,000 bonus miles. Charge everything: groceries, gas, dry cleaning, college tuition, airline tickets, medical bills, and so on. Make $24,000 in annual charges.	**34,000**
Telephone. At&T True Rewards gives 10 miles for every dollar spent, if you spend at least $75 a month. Assume your monthly phone bill is $100. Annual expense is $1,200. Switching long-distance telephone carriers can award 5,000 miles in addition to "deposits" for telephone usage.	**12,000**
Home Mortgage. Assume you re-finance a $250,000 home mortgage at 8 percent interest. Some lending home institutions will award mileage on the interest paid. For example, California Federal and Great Western Bank award one American Airlines AAdvantage mile for every dollar paid in interest.	**19,924**
Home improvements. Many home service companies offer mileage awards. For example, Brink's Home offer Security, True GreenChemlawn Yard, Merry Maids, and others. Spend $1,200 a year.	**1,200**

Music. Spend $200 a year with music clubs or retailers that offer mileage, such as 1-800-MUSIC-NOW, a division of MCI. It offers five miles for every dollar spent.

1,000

Magazines. Earn 500 to 1,000 miles for subscriptions to qualifying magazines that offer mileage, such as Business Week.

1,500

Take a vacation. Let's assume you fly and earn 2,000 miles on your airline of choice and earn 1,500 from your hotel. We're assuming a family of four. Assume a $300 per person ticket. Use the Delta SkyMiles card and earn 1 1/2 miles for every dollar spent on airfare. Earn triple miles on your rental car.

6,800

Business travel. Assume five trips per year with average round-trip miles of 1,500 per trip and an average cost of $500 per ticket. Charge your company travel on your card, if possible, and get reimbursed so that you earn the mileage credit. Rental cars typically earn 500 miles per rental, and hotels usually award 500 miles per stay. Car rental companies typically run promotions offering double and triple miles. Assume only two of the five rentals is during a promotion. Assume only one hotel is offering double miles.

17,500

Charitable donations. Many charitable organizations will award miles for your donations. More than 20 charities make awards, including the March of Dimes, National Audubon Society, the Alzheimer's Association, Goodwill Industries, and others. The Jewish National Fund offers double miles for first time donors. The SDMS Educational Foundation in Dallas gives 2,000 miles for a $200 donation. Assume $500 in annual donations.

500

TOTAL MILES EARNED
134,624

Now, what are you going to do with all your miles? Redeem them for FREE airline tickets or a FREE cruise? Throw in a FREE car and FREE hotel stay? Your choice!

Award redemption levels vary from airline to airline, but as a general rule, award levels require the following mileage:

Free ticket to anywhere in the 48 states   20,000 - 25,000 miles
Free ticket to Hawaii   30,000 - 35,000 miles
Free ticket to Europe   50,000 miles

Just for using your credit card instead of check or cash, you have earned six domestic tickets, four tickets to Hawaii, or two, almost three, tickets to Europe. Use of credit cards requires discipline. If you get whacked over credit card usage, bag the miles and lower your stress! But for me, I'll use my cards and earn free travel.

Yeah, I know you may never charge that much to your card because you don't make that much money! (That's why you're reading this book, to save big money!) So how about a scenario for us humble folks?

Here's a scaled down version that almost anyone can make. A new card bonus: 5,000 (you get 5,000 for the "regular" card and 10,000 for a Gold card); dining out: 12,000 ($100 per month earning 10 miles for every dollar spent); charge everything: 9,600 ($800 per month, charging everything you previously had written a check or paid cash for); magazine subscriptions: 500; travel: 5,600 (two airline tickets a year averaging $300 each, average air mileage of 2,000 per ticket, and $1,000 in travel related costs, such as hotel, car, admission, attractions, etc.). This is a fairly modest approach. Guess what you earned? 32,700 miles! That's enough for a ticket anywhere in the 48 states or to Hawaii. Now, suppose you don't travel at all this year? Let's subtract the 5,600 miles then. What's left? 27,100 miles. It's still enough for a free ticket anywhere in the 48! Frequent flyer programs are not just for frequent flyers!

How Do *YOU* Redeem Frequent Flyer Miles?
Well, I guess that's up to you.
Here's how others redeem their frequent flyer mileage.[11]

Free personal flights	84%
Free business flights	23%
Hotels stays	10%
Gifts	9%
Upgrades	5%
Car Rentals	1%

Total exceeds 100% due to multiple responses.

The competition between credit card companies for your business is intense. Many will include special offers to entice you into their fold, including low interest rates, free merchandise, and free travel. For example, at present, American Citibank AAdvantage cardholders who upgrade their

VISA card to a Gold card, or new members who become gold cardholders receive a free companion ticket on American Airlines. Cardholders will receive an additional companion ticket certificate with every 14 segments (flights) or 15,000 miles flown on tickets charged to the card. To upgrade your current Citibank card to a Gold card, call 800-950-5114. To apply for a Citibank card, call 800-359-4444. (I enrolled in American's AAdvantage two months ago and just received an invitation to apply for a Citibank VISA card and receive the buy one, get one free American ticket offer. It seems to have been sent automatically upon my AAdvantage enrollment.)

Are you planning to buy or sell a house? You can earn up to 40,000 TWA miles if you buy or sell your house through Better Homes and Gardens Realty. To earn the miles, you must enroll before listing or buying your home. Call 800-325-4815 to enroll.

Delta SkyMiles has teamed up with American Express for a new credit card that awards new cardholders 5,000 bonus SkyMiles and 10,000 SkyMiles for new Gold card members. This card also gives you one and half times your actual flown mileage award on Delta when your tickets are paid for with the card. To enroll, call 800-SKY-MILE.

Here are some dining programs that offer mileage awards. These are not credit cards. They are dining award programs that earn you frequent flyer miles. You may remit with your choice of payment. I suggest you use your airline affinity credit card and earn miles for using your credit card in addition to the dining program miles.

Alaska Airlines DineAir program. Awards three miles per dollar spent at participating restaurants in California, Oregon, and Washington. Call 800-207-8232 to enroll.

American Airlines AAdvantage Dining. Awards three miles per dollar spent at participating restaurants. Gold and Platinum members are automatically enrolled. Other AAdvantage members can enroll at 800-267-2606.

Delta Air Lines SkyMiles Dining. Awards three miles for every dollar spent at participating restaurants. To enroll, call 800-346-3341.

Northwest Airlines WorldPerks Dining. Awards two miles for every dollar spent at participating restaurants, with a $25 minimum purchase. To enroll, call 800-447-3757.

TWA and Dining A La Card. Awards 10 miles for every dollar spent with Dining A La Card at participating restaurants. The first 60 days of membership are free, thereafter a $49.95 annual fee is charged. To enroll, call 800-325-4815.

United Airlines Mileage Plus Dining. Awards 10 miles for every dollar spent at participating restaurants. To enroll, call 800-555-5116.

Although unusual, it does happen that an airline, cruise line, or other travel supplier will unexpectedly declare bankruptcy, suspend or cease operations, or otherwise go out of business. You may be offered some measure of protection against financial loss if your purchase was made with a credit card. In some circumstances, you can deny payment inasmuch as the services and products charged were never received. Check with your card provider for details.

Airline Elite Status

Airline	Service Number	Elite Status	Requirements
Alaska *Mileage Plan*	800-654-5669	MVP	15,000 miles on Alaska or Horizon.
		MVP	25,000 miles on Alaska, Horizon, and/or Northwest, or 30 segments on these airlines.
		MVP Gold	45,000 miles on Alaska, Horizon, and/or Northwest, or 60 segments on these airlines.
America West *FlightFund*	800-247-5691	Chairman's Club	20,000 miles.
		Master's Club	50,000 miles.
American *AAdvantage*	800-882-8880	Gold	25,000 miles or 30 segments.
		Platinum	50,000 miles or 60 segments.
		Top Platinum	By invitation only.
Continental *OnePass*	800-621-7467	Bronze	20,000 miles or 25 segments.
		Silver	35,000 miles or 40 segments.
		Gold	50,000 miles or 60 segments.

Delta *Frequent Flyer*	800-323-2323	Medallion	25,000 miles or 30 segments.
		Gold	50,000 miles or 60 segments.
		Platinum	100,000 miles or 100 segments.
Northwest *WorldPerks*	800-327-2881	Preferred Gold	25,000 miles. 60,000 miles.
Southwest *Rapid Rewards*	800-445-5764	No elite levels.	
TWA *Frequent Flyer* *Bonus*	800-325-4815	White Gold	5,000 miles. 20,000 miles or 4 trans-Atlantic segments.
		Red	40,000 miles or 8 trans-Atlantic segments.
United *Mileage Plus*	800-421-4655	Premier	25,000 miles or 30 segments.
		Executive Premier	50,000 miles or 60 segments.
		100,000 Mile Flyer	100,000 miles or 100 segments.
USAir *Frequent* *Traveler*	800-872-4738	Gold	25,000 miles.
		Gold Plus	50,000 miles.

My favorite credit cards for earning airline frequent flyer miles are American Express, using the American Express Membership Miles program, and Diners Club.

Frequent Flyer Elite Status. Airlines reward their best customers with elite frequent flyer status. The typical perks of belonging to this group are upgrades, advance boarding of aircraft, preferred seating, bonus miles, and other benefits in addition to the actual mileage flown.

Insider Tip: Want to hang out with the big guys? American Airlines offers a little known program that can accelerate your qualification for elite status called Top Tier Quick Qualifying. American AAdvantage requires 25,000 miles or 30 segments to qualify for Gold status, and 50,000 miles or 60 segments to become a Platinum member. (The Top Platinum invitation is issued by the top execs at American to those travelers who practically "live" on American Airlines. The frequency of travel, class of service, and the amount you spend on air travel with American are the primary criteria.)

The Top Tier Quick Qualifying program can award you Gold status if you fly 8,000 miles in a 90-day period. Platinum status can be awarded if you fly 16,000 miles in a 90-day period. That's 8,000 miles instead of 25,000, and 16,000 miles instead of 50,000.

Notice I said you "can" be awarded a Gold and Platinum elite status. Obviously, American is not interested in creating shortcuts that undermine AAdvantage. The program is designed to "hook" a potential frequent traveler and get them into the American family...and flights. The offer to participate is at the discretion of American Airlines.

This program is not available to any AAdvantage members who have previously attained Gold or Platinum levels. If granted, it is a one-time only offer, and probably would not be extended to AAdvantage members who have a zero mileage balance. In other words, this is for someone who is serious about flying American Airlines and the carrier wants to say "thank you" and "come again." Contact the American Airlines AAdvantage Customer Service Department at 800-882-8880 to determine if you might qualify for enrollment, and then get going!

A interesting side note on becoming a Gold or Platinum AAdvantage member is that other airlines including Continental, Delta, Northwest, and United will match your American status with their respective elite status. To be granted matching status, you will be required to submit proof of your elite status, such as a mileage statement, card, or letter stating your level, to the other airline. Larry's Law: Use it, but don't abuse it!

INTERNET AND LAST-MINUTE SALES. With the expansion of Internet use, several airlines have introduced bargain sales for last-minute travel. Airlines' yield management departments calculate what routes may be "soft." Then, to help fill their planes, they offer discounts up to 90 percent off. At present, seven airlines offer last-minute discount fares through the Internet. Typically, the fares are listed on Wednesday, departures are on Saturday (three days later) and return flights are the following Monday or Tuesday. Listed below are current Internet airline offers:

America West's "Deal of the Week." Prices are reduced up to 40 percent off advertised fares. Hotel information and pictures, itineraries and points of interest in Arizona, California, Florida, Nevada, Canada, and Mexico are listed. *http://www.americawest.com*

American Airlines NetSAAver fares. Currently, most departures are from Chicago and Dallas, but other cities are sometimes included. In time, more and more cities will be added. Click on NetSAAver, subscribe to the free service, and you will receive an e-mail list of fares each week. You can also call American at 800-344-6702 and request the fares. *http://www.americanair.com*

Carnival Air Lines Cyberdeals. Carnival's "Cyberdeals" are posted on the carrier's Web site each week and are not advertised elsewhere. *http://www.carnivalair.com*

Continental Airlines COOL fares. The site provides basic information on flight schedules, destinations, and route maps. You can even send an e-mail postcard to anyone with an e-mail address at the Wish You Were Here Section. Sign up at the "Flying the Net" section for Continental's On-Line (COOL) Travel Specials, which is an e-mail service that will alert travelers to special discounts. *http://www.flycontinental.com*

Northwest Airlines Cybersaver fares. Exclusive online fares and other information includes weather, flight schedules, arrivals, and departures. You can also check your Northwest frequent flyer account. *http://www.nwa.com*

Trans World Airlines. Fares can be booked up to a month in advance. Discounts will run to 75 percent off full-coach fares. *http://www.twa.com*

USAir E-Saver Discounts. For Boston, Philadelphia, and Pittsburgh departures. You will receive, via e-mail, a weekly list of specials. USAir will shortly expand the program to other cities. *http://www.usair.com*

Silent Auctions. American, Cathay Pacific, and Aer Lingus have used the Internet for on-line "silent auctions" where you submit an e-mail "bid" for tickets. American posted offers for travel to nine U.S. destinations. Cathay Pacific (*http://www.cathay-usa.com*) auctioned 387 round-trip tickets from New York City and Los Angeles to Hong Kong in Coach, Business, and First Class. The minimum bid was only $300. Tickets were sold at up to 50 percent regular fares. Aer Lingus (*http://www.aerlingus.ie*) sold tickets from the United States to Ireland with a minimum bid of only $200 round-trip. Tickets sold for about 50 percent off the regular fares.

You can expect more airlines to jump on this bandwagon. Surf the airline Web sites and you may find some real bargains!

Listed below are some additional Internet addresses. At present, however, the airlines do not offer cyber fares.

Alaska Airlines	http://www.alaska-air.com
Aloha Airlines	http://www.alohaair.com/aloha-air
Delta Air Lines	http://www.delta-air.com
Frontier Airlines	http://www.cuug.ab.ca:8001/~ busew/frontier.html
Hawaiian Airlines	http://www.hawaiianair.com
Southwest Airlines	http://www.iflyswa.com
United Airlines	http://www.ual.com
Valujet	http://www.valujet.com
Western Pacific	http://www.westpac.com

Although not yet available online, Delta Air Lines' **Escape Plan** offers bargain weekend fares from Cincinnati and Atlanta for SkyMiles members (Delta's frequent flyer program). Other cities may be added shortly. There is an $89 enrollment fee. Enrollment is limited. Discounts run up to 60 percent off normal published advance purchase fares. Six destinations are offered each week. There are no black-out dates. Domestic departures are Friday and Saturday, returning Sunday and Monday. In November, new international destinations will be offered with longer stays available. Hotel and car rental specials are also available. Call Delta at 800-895-2005 for more information and/or enrollment. I think the Escape Plan may be added to online members soon.

Most major foreign carriers maintain a Web site. You can usually find their location, even if you don't know their address, by listing their name or initials after "www" or enter the carrier's name in a search. Check their pages from time to time and find out what specials are being run. It is not only fun, it can save you a lot of money.

Best Ways To Get An Upgrade	
Experienced Travelers Reveal Their Secrets![12]	
Frequent Flyer Program	71%
Friendly with airline staff	19%
Travel agency influence	13%
Business contacts with airlines	12%
Social contacts with airlines	8%
Other	2%
Total exceeds 100% due to multiple responses.	

Creative Airline Ticket Summary

In short, creative ticketing is the key to discount travel and savings. This epistle is not intended to answer every question or identify each and every method of reducing your airfare. Rather, its purpose is to stimulate your mind to the concept of creative ticketing. The information we have reviewed is a thumb nail sketch of what is available to you.

We have talked about 16 basic principles of saving travel dollars:

- Planning ahead
- Knowing the lingo
- Be flexible
- Fare Wars
- Promotions and discount coupons
- Consolidator tickets
- Alternate city tickets
- Back-to-back tickets
- Breaking the fare, also known as split ticketing
- Point beyond fares
- Buying a round-trip ticket, even if you are only traveling one-way, if the round-trip fare is less expensive
- Special circumstance tickets: senior, bereavement, military, group, compassion, etc.
- Children's fares
- Student and youth fares
- Credit cards and frequent flyer awards
- Internet sales

Caveat emptor! "Let the buyer be aware." Some airlines and many travel agencies are not likely to be up to date on the art of creative discount travel. Airlines will only tell you about their fares, even though their respective fares may be higher than the competition. Most airline reservation agents are not knowledgeable on creative ticketing methods. Travel agencies perform a valuable service and will do *their* best to find you a bargain. Unfortunately, travel agencies simply are not trained or staffed to "bird dog" all the discount specials that are hitting the market every day. If you doubt me, go back to Chapter One and identify all the discount offers listed there that your travel agent informed you about. Remember that list, which you may think is long, is really quite short. It's only the tip of the iceberg of what is available. And, unfortunately, what you don't know can hurt you....or at least hurt your wallet.

So how can you keep up on the many deals and bargains that come on the market every day? Well, I told you earlier there are only two ways for you to get this information. You can be your own Dick Tracy, or have some-one do it for you. Remember, find a street smart travel guy who finds a challenge in ethically and legally beating the system.

Chapter 4
Travel Clubs

Few things in life are as exciting as travel. We all dream of visiting far away places, seeing the wonders of the world, and enjoying new experiences. Travel clubs can help you fulfill your dreams at a fraction of the cost others pay.

What is a travel club? A travel club is an organization that provides travel services and opportunities to its members. Some clubs provide real value, others are a sham and their owners should be locked up! I'll show you how to evaluate a travel club and decide if it's right for you.

I have been intrigued by travel clubs and have spent the last year researching, examining, probing, interviewing, analyzing, and dissecting just about every travel club I could find in America! With my eyes closed and my hands tied behind my back, I can tell you just about anything you want to know about travel clubs, both the good and the bad.

There are three primary types of travel clubs:

Travel Club #1. A membership organization whose *primary* purpose is to provide top travel values and special opportunity travel deals that may not always be available to the general public.

Travel Club #2. A membership organization whose *primary* purpose is selling overpriced memberships. Travel is offered, but seems to be of secondary importance to collecting dues and fees.

Travel Club #3. A membership organization whose *primary* purpose is to sell travel agent identification cards to non-travel agents promising that you will receive a host of travel agent benefits. (Yes, there is a sucker born every minute!) The pitch here is that you can suddenly become a "travel agent" and travel for almost nothing! The pitch is a myth.

Let me review each one briefly, starting with Clubs #2 and #3. All of these "travel club" organizations are built around the concept and premise of travel. I think the organizers of Clubs #2 and #3 picked travel simply because it is perceived to be exciting, sexy, and glamorous. The excitement clouds the reality. Unfortunately, our hearts do the buying, not our heads!

Travel Club #2 sells travel to its members. It usually promises a split of the travel agency commissions on your travel and the travel of your referrals. (Travel agencies typically receive 5-10 percent of the selling price of an airline ticket, cruise, hotel, tour package, etc.) I've seen these "clubs" offer up to 40 percent of the commission. I've never met anyone who actually received 40 percent. Most people I've spoken with didn't receive anything. The big push is to sell memberships, which cost anywhere from $1,000 to $5,000. *The emphasis is on selling memberships, not selling travel.* The real benefit to members are the commissions on selling memberships. Some of these "clubs" will eventually collapse under their own weight. The "front end" organizers make millions (literally and monthly!). Early members may sell a lot or a little and they may make some money, too; but eventually, thousands of people will get burned. Travel Club #2 will talk to you about travel, but the sizzle is selling memberships, not selling travel. You'd do better to take your money to Las Vegas and put it all on Black 28! At least the odds are better! It appears to be more of a money scheme than a travel club. *Caveat emptor!*

Travel Club #3 wants to make every member a "travel agent." "If you pay me enough money, I will call you a travel agent, travel counselor, or the Man in the Moon. I'll give you an ID card with your picture and something about travel printed on it and then promise you countless travel bargains 'available only to travel agents.'" You will hear testimonials of being upgraded on flights, discount hotel rooms, discount cruises, discount car rentals, and so on. Sorry, I forgot.... yes, you will talk about referring your friends who may want to become "travel agents," too. You will be told that you can make a good income—just give the club *your* money first!

Just a few weeks ago I was speaking at a convention. My topic was travel, of course. After my talk, the convention group was recessed for a break. I spoke individually with many people from all over the country, including a woman from Las Vegas. She asked me about a particular travel club she was about to join. The enrollment was a whopping $5,000 and she had pretty well made up her mind to join. After all, she would receive 30 percent of the commissions the club earned from travel she would "sell" or refer. She would also receive her "travel agent ID card" that would allow her all sorts of "free this" and "free that." She asked if I thought it was a good idea.

Well, I got out my pocket calculator and asked her, "Okay, how much travel do you really think you can sell out of your home?"

She replied, "With all the people I know, maybe 10 tickets a month."

"Fine," I said, "The average ticket cost in the country is around $250. Let's assume you do 10 tickets a month. That's $2,500 worth of tickets monthly and $30,000 annually. Not bad." She was smiling at the prospect of all this money she would earn.

"Let's figure out your commission. First, subtract the 10 percent tax because no commission is paid on taxes. That leaves $2,250 a month and $27,000 a year. The agency, in most situations, will collect a 10 percent commission. They keep 7 percent and give you 3 percent, right?"

"That's right," she said.

"Okay, that means you pay $5,000 and will earn $67.50 a month and $810 a year. Suppose you double your ticket volume. Now you earn $135 a month and $1,620 a year. And we haven't even figured in the lost interest amount on your so-called investment."

"Well, I really am not joining to make money."

"No, then what are you doing it for?"

"The perks."

"The what?"

"The perks. The travel perks. I get a travel agent ID card and can travel for free. [Now being a travel agent myself, I do wish this were true!] I figure I can get my money back in free tickets and cruises."

Never wanting to burst any bubble of hope, but feeling a need for the truth, I took my real travel agent ID out of my wallet and showed it to her. "When this company was making their presentation to you and asking you for $5,000, did they show you what their travel agent ID card looked like?"

"They had a picture of one," she replied.

"Well, let me tell you about travel agent cards. They are called IATAN Travel Agent ID cards and they are not issued by any travel agency, but by the IATAN [International Airline and Travel Agent Network] governing body. I have seen this company's ID cards and they are not the real thing. They have your picture on it, the travel agency's name and number, but that's about it. Go back and ask them point blank, 'Is the card that I will receive an IATAN card?' That is a 'Yes' or 'No' question. Then ask them to explain the airline rules governing free and reduced rate travel. Have them explain what is required by most carriers, namely, 6 to 12 months of employment *before* taking a flight, 35 or more hours every week, and salary requirements."

"They didn't talk about any of that stuff."

My parting advice, "Pass on this one. There are some excellent travel clubs out there, but this just *ain't* one of them!"

The primary emphasis of this pitch is selling phony ID cards. At first, some of these "card mill" companies sold bogus cards. Several law suits cooled their heals. Now, they sell "look alike" travel agent ID cards. You pay anywhere from $495 to $5,000 for membership in Travel Club #3 and then you are instructed on how to tell airlines, hotels, cruise lines, etc. that *you* really are a travel agent. (Reminds me of the high school boy who buys a phony driver's license so he can buy beer. As if having an ID that said he was 21 somehow magically made him 21!) Here's the rub, they tell you that you really are a travel agent and therefore qualify! Here's the test:

→ Ask if the ID card is an IATAN card. An IATAN card is the official and universally recognized travel agent ID. The IATAN card is not issued by a travel agency, but by the IATAN international governing body. There is no substitute. The card is either an IATAN card or it is not. Period!

→ Ask for a copy of the eligibility requirements for receiving free and reduced travel issued by any major airline, say.....Delta Air Lines, American Airlines, and United Airlines. Don't accept some weird story about why this doesn't really apply....you're being lied to if they say it does not.

→ Ask them to explain the length of employment, minimum hours required working as a travel agent, and minimum compensation required for travel benefits.

Well, enough said. Bottom line, the big money is made by those selling memberships and "phony" ID cards. The pitch to you is to sell your friends and presto, they're suddenly travel agents, too. Just remember you will have to face these people when it all crashes!

There is a legitimate business opportunity for those interested in pursuing a full or part-time career in travel. There are several quality programs that allow you to "set up shop" in your home and book or refer business to your sponsoring travel agency. To help determine the legitimacy of these "biz ops," ask yourself where the emphasis is. Is it on travel? Or on money making schemes by selling others the "biz op?" What training will you receive? What support systems are in place? Many people have established a good travel business starting part-time and either keeping it part-time or growing it into a full-time profession.

Travel Club #1 is where you'll find the real travel deals. Let's talk about what makes a good travel club:

- The primary emphasis is on travel.
- There are membership fees. A good travel club *must* charge dues to provide its unique services. The cost of membership is not outrageous. Usually membership fees run around $75-$150.
- If you introduce friends to the club, you should receive some benefit if they join. The benefit is reasonable and fair in relation to the cost of membership.

- The club will provide a constant flow of information, like what I teased you with in Chapter One, "Travel Deals Are Everywhere!" It's much more than just selling travel, it is providing a tidal wave of information. Remember, the *emphasis* is on travel. It is perfectly okay to offer incentives to refer your friends to the program (there are savings in numbers), but the *emphasis* is on legitimate travel opportunities.
- **STOP! Special Travel Opportunity Purchases!** A good travel club will offer travel bargains that are not always available to the general public, such as special airfares, cruise prices, hotel rates, and other valuable services to travelers.
- Airline Discounts. What discounts below the "lowest published fare" are available? A legitimate travel club will keep you informed.
- Hotel Discounts. Does the club provide a comprehensive hotel directory? A word of caution here. Many travel clubs offer great hotel rates that are only available when the hotel anticipates being "less than 80 percent full." I took the discount hotel book of several reasonably good travel clubs and tested them. Yes, the discounts did exist. No, the rates were not always available. In one test, only one in ten hotels I called said the discount would be available and two of the ten hotels claimed they were not even aware of the discount program. (I think the latter problem is more a function of communication at the hotel than with the discount program.) Ask if the hotel rates are <u>always</u> available or just when the place is empty.
- Award system. Something along the lines of a Frequent Flyer program which will award you miles or points for *your* travel purchases and for the purchases of *your friends and referrals.*
- Money Back Guarantee. Absolutely, positively! An ethical club will unconditionally offer you your money back if you're not satisfied.
- Additional Member Benefits. A good club will offer a host of member benefits including all those listed above and a variety of others, such as discount coupon books, monthly newsletters, a membership user guide, and so on.

Why can travel clubs offer such good deals? Last year my partners and I sold our travel agency. We were one of the largest agencies in the country and, frankly, we offered some pretty good deals. I negotiated all contracts and "deals" with travel suppliers, which consisted of airlines, cruise lines, hotels, car rental companies, tour companies, and anyone and everyone who supplied a travel product or service.

I remember a vice president of a major cruise line coming to me and asking me to help him "move some inventory." Translated, this means "Lar, we've got some empty space on our ships, and I want you to move it. To do so, I'll give you a really low fare."

"Okay, tell me more."

"Well, there's just one catch. You can't advertise it."

"How then do you want me to inform people?"

"Word of mouth. Call previous customers. Just don't announce it or advertise it."

Of course, I knew this before he walked into my office because we had done this many times before. We sold cruises at a fraction of the brochure rate. Buy one, get one free; big discounts; third and fourth passengers cruise free. You name it, we did a deal together and moved some cabins.

Now, why didn't the cruise line want me to advertise? What would happen if a cruise that sold for $1,500 per person, were suddenly advertised at $499 per person? The very same cruise; the very same cabin. Can you imagine how many irate customers would be demanding a refund? The cruise line would go out of business if they deeply discounted all passengers. They wanted to fill their empty cabins, but had to do so quietly so as not to disrupt their traditional sales distribution channels. (Translation: those paying higher rates.)

Does this mean that the only cruise bargains are last-minute sales? No. Cruise lines, airlines, hotels, and car rental companies project sales based upon current market conditions and past historical sales data. On any given flight, an airline will forecast the number of seats they beleive will be sold and how many will go empty. A cruise line predicts the number of cabins that will be sold. A hotel estimates how many empty rooms it may have on any given night. Car rentals know how many idle cars will be on their lot each day. This is a function of **yield management**. Yield is the revenue that is generated by a sale. Travel suppliers manage their yield so as to have better and tighter controls over their inventory, viz., airline seats, cruise cabins, hotel rooms, and rental cars.

What will a travel supplier do to move some unsold inventory? Travel inventory is not like hard goods inventory that I can hold onto until the next day, week, or month. Travel is the most perishable of commodities. Airlines, cruise lines, hotels, and car rental companies are willing to negotiate and "deal" to move their product. But they don't want the world to know about it. (Especially the poor guy who paid $1,500 for the cruise that you only paid $499 for!) Travel suppliers also want to move inventory during "soft" periods. They do so with fare wars, sales, and other incentives. They also talk privately with organizations, such as travel clubs, that can "quietly" move it for them.

If airline seats, cruises, hotel rooms, car rentals, etc. can be offered to a "closed membership organization," this becomes the ultimate "cover" for travel suppliers. They know that a travel club or other private organizations will sell only to their members and they can explain away the discount, if they have to, by saying that the special rates were not available to the general public.

Airlines may approach a travel club and ask the club to "move market share." Translation, "Give me a disproportionate share of your business and I will give your club and its members discounts that I don't want the whole world to know about!" The same is true with hotels and car rentals.

Do I recommend joining a travel club? A qualified yes. I see so many good people get taken in by Clubs #2 and #3. Sooner or later, they will probably get burned. Here is a checklist for evaluating a travel club.

Travel Club Membership Checklist:
Does this travel club:

_____ 1. Talk more about travel or about making money from selling memberships than about travel?

_____ 2. Charge a membership fee that is unreasonable?

_____ 3. Tell me that somehow I will become a travel agent with an ID card?

_____ 4. Tell me I will get fabulous travel benefits by showing my ID and telling people I am a travel agent when I'm not?

_____ 5. Suggest I sell my friends travel agent ID cards and make them travel agents, too?

Caution: If you answered "yes," to *any* of the above questions, please be careful and reconsider. My experience is that these programs lack substance and you may get burned. These are travel Clubs #2 and #3.

Let's continue with our checklist. If you are interested in travel Club #1, ask these questions; does the club:

_____ 6. Offer a comprehensive hotel discount program and directory?

_____ 7. Offer hotel discounts applicable at all times or just some times?

_____ 8. Book me an airline ticket at rates less than the lowest published fare? (It is unreasonable to expect this on every ticket, but can you get it on some tickets?)

_____ 9. Give me a discount coupon book that offers reduced rates on theme parks, attractions, restaurants, etc.?

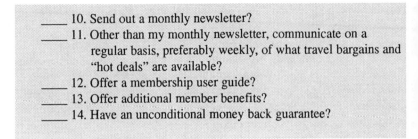

_____ 10. Send out a monthly newsletter?
_____ 11. Other than my monthly newsletter, communicate on a
regular basis, preferably weekly, of what travel bargains and
"hot deals" are available?
_____ 12. Offer a membership user guide?
_____ 13. Offer additional member benefits?
_____ 14. Have an unconditional money back guarantee?

If you answered "yes" to questions 6-14, then go ahead and consider joining. A good, legitimate travel club will save you a ton of money. Like any other business, there are good ones and not so good ones. As we discussed earlier, the emphasis must be on travel. It's okay to have opportunities to make some money in the travel business, but the core business of a travel club must be travel and providing discounts and travel values to its members. In fact, if you even travel infrequently, you can save your membership fee many times over.

You should consider a reasonable membership fee, usually somewhere between $75 and $150, as a plus, *not* a negative. With the recent commission cap imposed by airlines on travel agents (airlines placed a maximum cap on how much a travel agency can earn in airline ticket commissions), many travel agencies are charging service fees, which may run from $5 to $10 per ticket. Those agencies that do not now charge client fees, may be forced to soon. Any travel club you are considering joining must have a timely way to communicate with you on what deals are breaking. A monthly newsletter is good, but won't get the job done because travel bargains don't wait for printing deadlines. Preferably, you will receive a weekly fax, e-mail, or some form of communication. Knowledge is power!

Can I recommend a travel club? Yes. There are several good ones. I have listed some of them at the end of this chapter. My personal recommendations are Travel Connections and the Columbus Travel Club. Both Travel Connections and the Columbus Travel Club answer "no" to questions 1-5, and "yes" to questions 6-14.

In evaluating a travel club, remember the emphasis must be on travel and it must specifically identify the member benefits listed in questions 6-14. Ask if you will receive a fax or other communication in between monthly newsletters that will notify you of specials as they break. If you only get notification once a month of the "hot deals," you will know about it two or three weeks after it hits the market. Often by that time space is sold out.

In addtion to those features mentioned in questions 6-14, look for additional member benefits, including:

- A Frequent Flyer award program that not only rewards you miles or points for your travel purchases, but also gives you points for the travel of others that you refer to the club.
- Discount dining program that will save you 10-50 percent.
- A signing bonus. Pro athletes get a signing bonus. Why not travel club members? Your signing bonus can take the form of Frequent Flyer Miles or special discounts. Some travel clubs will give all new members a free hotel/resort stay. Another club gives all new members a camera.
- Discount directory for golf or tennis.
- A money back guarantee!

Listed below are some travel clubs. All numbers are toll-free.

Columbus Travel Club	800-373-3328
Encore Travel	800-444-9800
Travelers Advantage	800-548-1116
Travel Connections	888-745-4110

Chapter 5

Cruises
Don't Get Soaked

Ah-h-h-h-h! I love cruising. There are few pleasures in life more enjoyable than watching the waves glide by over an endless stretch of blue ocean and then mysteriously appearing in some exciting, foreign port of call. The mind and body are refreshed and the senses are awakened! Cruising is consistently the best travel bargain.

Cruise Capers
Things to Remember When Buying a Cruise

- Know how to *Shop Smart!*
- **NEVER, NEVER, NEVER PAY THE BROCHURE RATE!**
- All cruises are not created equal. There is a tremendous difference between cruise lines and even among ships within the same cruise company. Cruise experiences range from budget to deluxe and every thing in between.
- Don't rely on the brochure photos, especially when it comes to cabin size and design. Talk with an experienced cruise agent about the comfort of your stateroom.
- Carefully read the brochure information pages, particularly the Terms and Conditions, which include details regarding deposits, insurance, and cancellation penalties.
- Whenever possible, book early. Always ask for an early booking and/or early payment discount.
- Ask regarding special promotions and discounts.
- Ask regarding 3rd and 4th passenger discounts, kids cruise free, guaranteed upgrades, on-board shopping credits, and so on. What's the key? You got it, "Always ask!"

- Ask for discounts for repeat customers.
- Know what is negotiable.
- Know the discount "code words."

Let the guy in the next cabin pay the brochure rate. There's no need for you to. The number of cruise bargains and discounts is increasing. Know what you're buying. Don't just compare prices. Evaluate the cruise line, ship, and itinerary. Two ships on the same itinerary operated by the same cruise line may be priced differently. **Shop *value*, not just price!**

Let's discover how to *Shop Smart* for your cruise.

Shop Smart
Steps to Buying a Cruise

Follow these steps religiously and you will *Shop Smart* and save a fortune on your next cruise:

Budget. Before looking at the brochures and getting yourself all worked up, sit down and determine a realistic budget. Remember my best travel advice. When getting ready to travel, don't overpack. Set all your clothes in one pile and all your money in another pile. Then, cut your clothes pile in half and double your money pile!

Establish a budget you can afford. Maybe you will later want to adjust it a little up or down, but begin with a budget in mind. Don't forget to include shore excursions, gratuities, and gifts.

Dates. Some people will go whenever a "hot" deal comes along. The time of year or cruise itinerary doesn't make a difference as long as it's a great price. For others, their cruise window is shorter and time sensitive. Typically the best values are in spring and fall.

Personality Match. Every cruise line and individual cruise ship has its own unique personality. A ship's clientele may reflect that personality. A cruise line may cater to an older group, a younger crowd, families, or to the party crowd. What is your group? An experienced cruise counselor can help you with a good cruise match. Cruise lines tend to target specific market segments or populations. Look at the pictures of the people in the cruise brochures. What market is that cruise line targeting? Can you identify and feel comfortable with the people in the cruise brochure photos and their activities?

Is your cruise more formal, semiformal, or casual? A formal cruise includes more formal evenings, tuxedos, cocktail dresses, "sophisticated" or upscale entertainment, and afternoon tea. Semiformal cruises are more relaxed. You won't see many tuxedos or evening gowns, but most gentlemen will wear a coat and tie to dinner with maybe one or two big dress-up evenings. Entertainment often involves musicals and stage productions. Casual cruises are probably the most popular. Some are very casual and laid back and others will involve some dress up, but there's no big push or pressure to conform to a coat and tie.

Cruise Itinerary. Read your cruise brochure. Review the itinerary. See what ports you will be landing in. Do these destinations appeal to you? You may want to do some research on the ports of call so that you can get the most out of your short visit. My wife and I recently took a 14-day cruise of the northern European capitals. We visited Copenhagen, Stockholm, Oslo, Tallin, St. Petersburg, Berlin, Amsterdam, and London. Many shore excursions were planned for each city. I researched each city, determined I could see on my own without joining a cruise organized shore excursion. We did our own self-guided tour, except in Estonia, Russia, and a train to Berlin, the latter we had the cruise ship arrange. We saw more and paid less. I arranged in advance of the cruise for a private car and guide in Tallin and St. Petersburg. There were four of us and the per person cost was less with a private car and guide than had we taken the shore excursions and tours offered by the cruise line.

Am I recommending that you do not take the tours and shore excursions offered by your cruise ship? No. They are well planned and you see the major sights, but you pay for it. If you are uncomfortable "winging" it on your own, sign up for the tours offered by the cruise line. Your research will also tell you which ports are well suited for walking around on your own and which are not. What's the lesson? Become familiar with your itinerary.

Some cruises sail into a new port each day. Other cruises offer mostly days at sea and open ocean. Most cruises offer a variety, which I like best. A few days at sea, then a port of call. The variety keeps life interesting. Your preference of ports of call to days at sea is an important consideration in your cruise selection.

Reading the Charts. Now look at the cruise prices. You will note, usually listed to the left of the rates, a list of letters that designate cabin or stateroom categories. Next to the cabin category letter is a description of the cabin. It will tell you which deck the cabin is located on, cabin bed arrangement, whether it's inside (windowless) or outside (portholes, windows, or verandah), and other information. You will usually see the sailing dates and a corresponding season, i.e., peak season, value season, or economy season.

Next, look at the deck-by-deck layout of the ship. The cabin categories are color coded for easy reference and list a cabin number. You can also see where all the public areas of the ship are located.

Choosing Your Cabin. Look at your cruise brochure for a specific ship and cruise itinerary. There are several decisions to make:

Cabin design. What is the bedding configuration? Square footage?

Inside cabin or outside cabin? Upper and lower berth? Two double beds? One queen or king bed? Portholes, windows, or private verandah? Study the brochure. Talk to your travel counselor. Refer to guide books on cruising.

Location. Generally, it is more comfortable to be mid-ship (center) than to be fore (front) or aft (rear) of the ship. The center provides less roll or movement. You will get less up and down movement on the waves. Mid-ship is also more convenient for getting around and is closer to elevators. The most desirable cabins are usually on the higher decks.

People often ask if I recommend booking an outside or inside stateroom. There is no right or wrong answer to this question. It is a matter of economics and personal preference. Some believe that the best approach is to get the most inexpensive cabin available because you don't spend that much time in it. Others believe that while you may not spend a lot of time there, having a window or verandah opens the room up and just makes the whole cruise experience so much more enjoyable. It's completely a personal preference and budget decision. If you can get a private verandah, you'll love it! It is worth the additional expense. It cannot be compared to an inside, windowless room. Personally, I always go for an outside stateroom.

Cabin Category Upgrades. As you review the cruise brochure, you will notice that each sailing has a wide variety of cabin categories. Always ask your booking agent if your particular sailing offers complimentary upgrades. The practice is quite common. This means you pay for a lesser priced cabin, but receive a much nicer cabin at no extra charge. I have seen complimentary cruise cabin upgrades go up six categories. Usually it is one or two categories. Always ask! Many travel agencies and travel clubs have contracts with cruise lines that provide guaranteed cabin category upgrades. It does matter who you book with!

Read the Fine Print. Read carefully and review with your travel agent the Terms and Conditions of your cruise. This section is usually found at the back of the brochure. Don't skip anything. Pay particularly close attention to the deposit, trip insurance, and cancellation policies.

Decisions! Decisions! and More decisions! After you have selected your cruise, you will have more decisions to make, including:

- **First or second dinner seating?** First seating is usually about 6:30 p.m. and second seating is about 8:30 p.m. Each cruise line will have their own time schedule.
- **Dining table.** Tables for two, four, six, and eight are usually offered. If you are traveling with friends, request a table to accommodate only your party. If you and your companion are not cruising with others, request a table for two, six or eight. Imagine getting a table for four and finding the other couple incompatible? It would make for a *very* long cruise.

Selecting A Cruise Line

Many factors affect your decision on which cruise line and ship you choose. Listed below are the 10 biggies of what goes into selecting a particular cruise (with #1 being the most important). The percentage indicates how many people in the survey listed that particular factor to be "very important."[13]

1. Ship's reputation for good passenger service............83%
2. General reputation of the cruise line.........................80%
3. Special discounts..78%
4. Ship's reputation for good dining and cuisine..........75%
5. Itinerary, ports of call to be visited.........................58%
6. Air/sea package availability.....................................55%
7. Quality of on-board entertainment...........................42%
8. Size of cabins..30%
9. Newness of the ship...28%
10. Size of the ship..25%

Survey results exceed 100% due to multiple responses.

Notice the importance of a cruise line's reputation. Of the top four responses, three dealt with reputation. Good individual service, general reputation for over-all good service, and fine dining. Right up there with reputation and service is price. Never, never, never pay the brochure rate!

Look at the percentage drop-off after the top four. I was somewhat surprised that cruise itinerary didn't rank higher. That's an important one to me.

- **Cancellation insurance.** All cruises carry cancellation penalties. The closer you get to the departure date, the more your cancellation will cost you. Cancellation insurance waives charges and penalties in most situations.
- **Special requests.** If you require a special diet, such as low fat, low sodium, kosher, vegetarian, etc., make your request at the time of booking. If you will be celebrating a special occasion, such as a birthday or anniversary, notify the cruise company through your travel agent when you make your reservation. If for any reason you forgot to mention your special request prior to the cruise departure, let your waiter or maitre d' know when you board.
- **Shore excursions.** In your cruise documents, you will receive a booklet describing tours offered in the ports of call. These are usually priced at a premium. You pay for the convenience. If you are

an adventurous type, hire a cab. There are always plenty waiting for arriving ships. Negotiate a half-day or full-day rate and see the sights on your own. It's nice to share the cab with another couple because it cuts the cost in half. Besides, the more the merrier! One of the most enjoyable shore excursions I remember was a full-day tour by taxi in Bermuda. We were traveling with another couple en route from New York City to St. Thomas, U.S. Virgin Islands by way of Bermuda. We landed ashore, spoke with several taxi drivers, and finally settled on one. We agreed upon a price and length of tour. The tour was a delight! We saw more and paid less than anyone else on the cruise ship!

Always negotiate the price before you get in the vehicle. Pay at the end of your tour, never at the beginning. I visited Elephanta Island, 10 km across the bay from Bombay, India. The four rock-cut temples were cut out between 450 and 750 AD. The most interesting sculpture shows Trimuti, or the three-headed Shiva, where he also takes the role of Brahma, the creator, and Vishnu, the preserver. As the ferry launch arrived at the island pier, we are descended upon by guides offering their services. I talked with several to gauge their knowledge, attitude, personality, language skills, and cost. We agreed not only on the price, but also on the length of our sightseeing tour. Many people forget to nail down the time and find they get short changed. We agreed on a two hour walking tour of the island and the caves. After an hour and 15 minutes, our guide saw another launch coming, told me the tour was over, and asked for payment. I paid him, but pro-rated the payment based on an hour and a quarter, rather than two hours. He asked about the full amount. I reminded him that he was leaving us early. He saw a boat load of tourists coming and hoped to take another tour rather than finish ours. He smiled and acknowledged that was true. He accepted the payment for his shortened tour and was even surprised when I tipped him. We shook hands and parted friends. What would have happened if I had paid him up front for the full two hours?

Use your own good judgement about who you hire and the car you will ride in. Trust your instincts. Talk to the driver and determine his language skills and local knowledge.

How to Get the Best Cruise Fare

Guaranteed Discount Rates. As I said previously, NEVER, NEVER, NEVER pay the cruise brochure rate! Here's the single most important insider secret to know about cruise fares. **Almost every cruise**

line has private, unpublished cruise rates. You need to know the **"code words"** that unlock a lower rate, often 50 percent or more below the brochure rate. These private rates are not available to every travel agent. Cruise lines quietly select who they will really deal with in a big way and who they will not.

For example, groups typically receive anywhere from a 20 to 50 percent discount. Does this mean that I must travel with some group to get a big discount? No. Many cruise lines offer group rates to individuals not traveling with a group. These are called **Guaranteed Group Rates.** The cruise company guarantees that you will receive a "group" discount even though you are traveling by yourself. This policy of discounting individual cruise passengers started by using group discounts. Now cruise lines use these private discounts, which are often lower than group discounts, as a means of filling their ships. Each cruise line has its own code words for the equivalent of a guaranteed group or similar discount. All discounts are based upon availability.

Here are some "**code words**":

Carnival	Super Saver Rates
Celebrity	Five Star Rates
Costa	Andiamo Rates[14]
Crystal	Advance Booking Rates and Guaranteed Group Rate[15]
Cunard	Multiple Rates[16]
Holland America	Saver Rates[17]
NCL[18]	Leadership Fares; Run of the Ship Rates[19]
Premier	See footnote[20]
Princess	Love Boat Savers
Radisson Seven Seas	See footnote[11]
RCCL[22]	Breakthrough rates
Seabourne	See footnote[23]

Here are two examples of cruise savings:

RCCL, *Majesty of the Seas*, seven-night Western Caribbean cruise.[24] (If I could pick my favorite seven-night Caribbean cruise itinerary, this is it.)

The per person, brochure rate for a Value Season sailing is:[25]

Inside cabins	$1,499 - $1,949	Categories Q - K
Outside cabins	$1,999 - $2,799	Categories I - B

This price includes the cruise and round-trip air from most cities in the United States. You will receive a $250 credit if you arrange your own air. Port taxes and fees are additional.

Here's what you won't see in the RCCL brochure: *Breakthrough* rates. *Breakthrough* is the code word for discounted prices on RCCL. Here are the *Breakthrough* prices for the very same sailing and cabin:

Inside cabins:	$849 - $ 949
Outside cabins:	$949 - $1,049

Your air transportation is not included, but is available for purchase from the cruise line or on your own. Just compare the airfares offered by the cruise line with what is available from your travel agent or travel club and take the best deal. The RCCL airfares are easy:

East	$279
Central	$329
West	$399

You can see that even if you take the RCCL air tickets, you have saved a considerable amount of money. If the current market price for air tickets is less than what is offered by RCCL, you save even more.

Here's another example: Princess Cruises, *Crown Princess*, seven-night Alaska sailing.[26] Let's pick cabin category GG, outside cabin. Here are the per person rates:

Brochure rate:	$2,349
Love Boat Savers rate:	$1,699 (30% discount)
Savings:	$ 700

This Princess savings is significant as Alaska cruise space is always tight. The season is only four months from mid-May to mid-September. Unlike other destinations, such as the Caribbean, that offer cruises year round, Alaska cruising must be packed into the summer months. In this case, if you **Shop Smart**, you receive a 30 percent discount. You receive exactly the same cruise, but have $1,400 per couple left on the table! (Don't ruin anyone's cruise by telling them what you paid!) P.S. I know of some Princess Alaska cruises in peak season discounted 50 percent off the brochure rate!

The names of discount programs differ from cruise line to cruise line, but the basic concept is still the same. A guaranteed discount. *A rose by any other name is still a rose!* Ask your booking agent for a guaranteed cruise discount and if a free upgrade is available. How do you ask without feeling funny about it? Try this approach, "What discounts off the brochure rate are available? Are any cabin upgrades available for this or other sailings?" It never hurts to ask!

Private Cruise Rates. Cruise lines typically make private deals and arrangements with travel clubs and agencies for private, not-to-be-talked about cruise rates. These special fares are even lower than the "code words" discussed. Yes, cruise lines have a "code word" name for these also; and yes, I know the code words. Sorry, I can't disclose them, but trust me, they exist. I've dealt with them for years. These private rates are unpublished and not available to the masses. If I were to publish the code words or discount names, it would create problems for cruise lines because those travel agents and travel clubs that don't have access to these lower priced, private rates would throw a fit. Typically, these private deals offer additional savings of $100-$300 per person on a one-week cruise; sometimes more and sometimes less.

You Asked It!

Here are some questions asked of Celebrity Cruises:[27]
"Does the elevator go to the front of the ship?"
"Why does the ship rock only when we are at sea?"
"Does the ship generate its own electricity?"
"Will I get wet if I go snorkling?"
"What do you do with the ice carvings after they melt?"
"Does the crew sleep on board?"
"Is there water all around the island?"
"What time is the midnight buffet?"
"Will trapshooting be held outside?"
"How will we know which photos are ours?"

Cruise Only vs. Air/Sea Option. In many cases, it is less expensive to purchase your cruise and air separately as opposed to a combined package deal that includes both. It is very easy to determine which is less expensive. Simply compare the cost of the airfare offered by the cruise line with what you can find on the market. If your air transportation is included in your cruise cost, ask what your credit is if you don't take the air transportation offered by the cruise line. If you have a street smart travel hustler in your corner, you will often do better on your airfare than what the cruise line will offer.

Always allow yourself more time than you think necessary to get to the ship. Cruise ships don't wait for passengers delayed en route to the departure port. Usually, when you supply your own air transportation, you must also provide your own transfers to the ship. This is really easy. No need for an expensive taxi since there are many companies offering shuttle services between the arrival airport and cruise departure pier. These shuttle transfers should be reserved in advance by your booking agent. Even when providing your own air, cruise lines usually will provide you with ship to airport transfers. Notify the purser or cruise travel coordinator on board the ship a few days prior.

Compare the rates and take the best one that suits you and your pocketbook. Ideally, your travel provider should be doing this for you.

Early Bird Discounts. Most cruise lines will offer a discount incentive for those who reserve and deposit six months or more in advance. The typical discount is five percent. Plan ahead and save!

Early Payment Discounts. Some cruise lines will discount your cruise if you pay in full six months or more in advance. This early payment discount is typically 5-10 percent.

Repeat Customer Discounts. Many cruise lines will offer additional discounts to repeat customers. For example, Crystal Cruises offers an additional five percent discount to "Crystal Society Members," which is anyone who has ever sailed with Crystal. Other lines offer similar discounts.

On-Board Discounts. Cruise lines usually have a "cruise counselor" onboard to help you with future cruise plans. You can put a refundable deposit on a future cruise. This on-board deposit entitles you to a five percent discount.

Can you combine discounts? Yes. Most cruise lines will allow you, for example, to combine an on-board discount, repeat customer discount, and early payment or early full payment discount. In addition to guaranteed group discounts, which can range from 20-50 percent, this strategy can yield an additional 15-20 percent discount.

What about these cruise coupons I see in discount books? In most cases, they're worthless. Even though they offer $50 to $100 per person discounts, the discount is usually applicable to full brochure rates which you now know you shouldn't be paying in the first place. There are a few coupons that are applicable to any cruise fare. Read the terms and conditions carefully.

Pre and Post-Cruise Stays. Inasmuch as you will most likely be flying to and from your cruise, you may wish to consider a few extra days on the front end or back end of your cruise vacation. Every cruise line will offer hotel options for you. In most cases, don't even think about taking them. Yes, it is convenient to have it all in one package. No, it's not always a good deal! In fact, it usually borders on robbery! The hotel rates offered in most cruise brochures are full "rack" rates, also known as the OUCH rate. Rarely can you do better booking the hotel through the cruise line than independently. Here, again, is where a good travel agent is worth his/her weight in gold. Your travel agent should be doing this and looking for the hotel deals that offer big discounts. The hotel deals are out there, you (no, your travel agent) just needs to know where to find them.

Cruising by Freighter, d.b.a....Off the Beaten Track! If you have time for a long adventure, consider sailing by freighter. Luxury it is not; clean and well kept it is. Exciting and adventurous? Well, that depends on you. Freighter travel is not for everyone. A *tourist* is better suited for a standard seven-day Caribbean cruise. A *traveler* will find freighter life a unique and exciting experience. You will forgo luxury, discos, Broadway shows, and nightlife for an adventure away from the crowds and into ports that see few outsiders. Remember, freighters are in the cargo business. Some may take passengers as a sideline. Your freighter itinerary is *always* subject to change, not only with respect to which ports you may call on, but even the length of the sailing may change a day or two. You must be flexible....and adventurous.

Here's the skinny on freighters. Most freighter travel is for voyages of 45 days or more. Freighters generally take you off the beaten track, or "off the familiar shore!" (Don't stop reading now, because I have a couple of dynamite two week freighter itineraries.)

The cost of freighter travel will average from $100+ per person, per

Which Is The Best Cruise Line?

That probably depends on who you're asking. Each cruise line has a different personality. One cruise line or particular ship may appeal more to you than another. Readers of two national travel magazines, *Travel & Leisure*[28] and *Condé Nast Traveler*,[29] picked their favorites and rated the cruise lines. Not surprisingly, the more expensive lines were on top. Here are the readers' favorites:

Travel & Leisure	*Condé Nast Traveler*
1. Crystal Cruises	1. Silversea Cruise Line
2. Seabourn Cruise Line	2. Seabourn Cruise Line
3. Windstar Cruises	3. Crystal Cruise Line
4. Radisson Seven Seas Cruises	4. Windstar Cruises
5. Holland America Line	5. Radisson Seven Seas Cruises
6. Celebrity Cruises	6. Cunard Sea Goddess Cruises
7. Princess Cruises	7. Holland America Line
8. Royal Caribbean Cruises Ltd.	8. Cunard Line
9. Cunard Line	9. Clipper Cruises
10. Renaissance Cruises	10. Special Expeditions

day and up. (The more exotic itineraries may cost more.) There is little price difference between freighter travel and the minimum cabin rates on vacation cruises. Freighter travel is a different mode of travel, not necessarily a less expensive one. Cabins are not luxurious, but clean and basic. Most cargo ships that carry passengers will have a library, reading area, and game room. Some even sport a swimming pool and exercise room. (A heck of a lot better than the *African Queen*, right?) Most freighters do not accept passengers. Those ships that do usually restrict the number of passengers to 12 or less, although there are a few which can take a large number of guests. Some even have an upper age limit, but most do not.

Although most freighter cruises last 45 days or more, here are two great itineraries that no vacation cruise line duplicates.

Bergin Lines cruises the Norwegian fjords on mail boats carrying 130 to 320 passengers. During your 12-day cruise, you will make as many as 30 to 35 stops in small coastal villages. The scenery is spectacular. Telephone 800-323-7436 or 212-986-2711.

Here's my favorite. The *Aranui* makes a 16-day run from Tahiti through the Tuamotu archipelago and north to the Marquesas Islands and return. You may stop at any of these isolated South Pacific islands. A recent journey took the *Aranui* from Tahiti to Takapoto, Ua Pou, Nuku Hiva, Hiva Oa, Fatu Hiva, Ua Huka, Rangiroa, and back to Papeete. Sometimes you may even make an unscheduled stop, such as a recent first time visit to Tahuata. Now, get your world atlas out and find this corner of paradise! These are islands where the natives, many of whom still live a traditional way of life, will come out to greet the *Aranui*. The ship is relatively small by freighter standards and can navigate her way through the coral reefs, atolls, and island groups. It is a step back in time. You will never see this itinerary nor these islands on a vacation cruise line.

For information regarding freighter cruises worldwide, contact:

Freighter World Cruises, 180 South Lake Drive, Pasadena, CA 91101. Telephone: 818-449-3106. F.W.C. serves as a general sales agent for several freight lines and publishes a twice monthly newsletter which features about 100 freighter cruises each month—several highlighted with commentary and notes. You can book your cruise with them and they will answer just about any question imaginable.

Ford's Freighter Travel Guide and Waterways of the World. This is a newsletter that is published quarterly and lists itineraries, accommodations, and rates. Available from Ford's Travel Guides, 19448 Londelius Street, Northridge, CA 91324. Telephone: 818-701-7414.

TravLtips is published monthly and lists freighter services, discounted trips, and general freighter information. The newsletter includes stories and reports from other members. Contact TravLtips, P.O. Box 188,

Flushing, NY 11358. Telephone: 800-872-8584 or 718-939-2400.

If you want to travel in style, book yourself on Ivaran Lines' *Americana*. This cargo ship will take about 100 passengers. The ship has an elegant four-story complex which includes a swimming pool, lounge area, gym, casino, beauty salon, and a pianist. The *Americana* sails out of New Orleans (Houston on occasion) to South America.

If you are interested in a unique experience, jump aboard a cargo ship and explore some new and exotic ports. If you need someone or something to entertain you 24 hours a day, freighter travel is not for you. If you enjoy the unusual, seeing new places, quiet and solitude, and the excitement of traveling off the beaten track, then sign on for a freighter cruise.

Cruise Consolidators. Cruise consolidators or discounters operate much the same way airline consolidators do. Cruise lines sell discounted sailings through consolidators and hope to fill empty cabins. Years ago, the difference between rates charged by cruise consolidators and travel clubs and travel agencies was significant. By and large, those days are over. There are many good cruise consolidators; some charge a fee, others do not. Here are a few:

Cruise Line	800-777-0707
Cruisc Pro	800-222-7447
	800-258-7447 California
	fax: 805-371-9084
Cruises, Inc.	800-854-0500
	fax: 315-434-9175
Cruises of Distinction	800-634-3445
	201-716-0088
	fax: 201-716-9893
World Wide Cruises	800-882-9000
	305-720-9000 Florida
	fax: 305-720-9112

Recommended Reading. All cruise brochures look great and promise you the time of your life; and most likely, you will have a great time! Especially if you *Shop Smart!* There are several cruise guidebooks that give an overview of ships and cruise lines.

Berlitz Complete Guide to Cruising and Cruise Ships. Douglas Ward. Macmillan Publishing.

Fodor's Cruises and Ports of Call. Fodor Travel Publications. Very good book that provides you details not only on your cruise ship, but a description of sights and attractions in major ports.

Frommer's Cruises. Marilyn Springer and Donald Schultz.

Prentice-Hall.

Cruise Lines International Association (CLIA) offers a free booklet that will answer many of your questions about cruises. The booklet is an information guide, not a discount source. The booklet *Cruising: Answers to Your Questions* is available free of charge from travel agencies and travel clubs that are CLIA members.

Post Script. Cruising is not only the best travel value on the market, it will probably be your most relaxing and exciting travel experience. *Shop Smart* and save! And send me a postcard!

Chapter 6
Hotels
And How To Avoid
A Nightmare!

Hotel ***Shop Smart*** is one of the greatest opportunities for travelers to save big money. Most people spend a lot of time looking to save every penny possible on airfares, yet give little attention to their hotel costs. In most cases, travelers will spend more money on lodging than on air transportation. It seems incongruent not to attack hotel rates with the same killer instinct one does airfares. In part, this may be due to the reality that it is easier to compare airfares than hotel rates.

What is a hotel rate? It is the price you are charged to stay at the property. ("Property" is a travel industry term for hotel and lodging.) What determines the price? Many factors influence rates, including competitive market conditions, location, cost of operation, demand, and so on. If a hotel tells you that the room charge is $150 a night, is there anything sacred about that amount? What it really means is that at this point in the conversation (negotiation), you can have the room for $150. What if you want to, or can afford to pay only $100? Suppose you offer the hotel $100 for the room they are asking $150 for? Well, the two options are fairly obvious:

Option 1:   The hotel can accept the lower amount, figuring $100 is
              better than an empty room, or

Option 2:   They can say "no."

If Option #1 is accepted, you save $50. If Option #2 is the answer, then you are still in a favorable position, you can:

- Say thanks and look elsewhere.
- Pay the $150 and get the room.
- Make a counter offer of, say, $125. Now the process starts all over again.

The point is there is nothing sacred about a rack hotel rate. (Dealing with hotel rates is much easier in person than over the telephone. I'll talk more about personally negotiating your room rate later.) The important lesson is to develop a frame of mind that you can have some control of your hotel costs. Do you remember we talked about airline yield management in Chapter Three? The same process takes place with hotels. The rates can float from day to day, even hour to hour, depending upon the occupancy rate. Obviously in slow or soft periods, hotels become very aggressive in filling their rooms. In peak periods, some hotels act as if they are doing you a favor to allow you to stay at their property and pay $250 a night! (Economics 101, Supply and Demand.)

Remember, there is a level where a hotel loses less by keeping a room empty than by renting it at any rate. There are variable costs and fixed costs in operating a hotel. If a hotelier believes he can rent some of his rooms that may otherwise go empty at rates lower than normal, he might do it provided he can do so without disrupting his normal sales and distribution

The Good Old Days

What a difference a few years make! Like everything else, hotel rates are not what they used to be! Here are some hotel rates in 1968 and what they are today.

San Francisco

The Fairmont Hotel:

1968 rates:	Singles started at $18, doubles at $23, and the Presidential Suite for only $150 per night.
1996 rates:	Mid-week singles start at $175 and suites start at $475 per night.

The Clift Hotel:

1968 rates:	Singles started at $17, doubles cost no more than $33, and suites went up to $65 per night.
1996 rates:	Singles start at $225 and doubles run from $270 to $370 per night.

Los Angeles

The Beverly Hilton:

1968 rates:	Singles were $16 to $28 per night, doubles ran $22 to $34.
1996 rates:	Singles are $185 to $260 per night, suites start at $400.

The Century Plaza Hotel:

1968 rates:	Singles started at $25 per night, suites cost $48 to $68 per night.
1996 rates:	Singles start at $150 per night, suites run $250 to $3,000.

channel of guests who pay the higher rates. The lower amount he gets for the discounted rate rooms are, in reality, incremental or extra income.

Hotel Discounts. Have you noticed that when you call a hotel for reservations, particularly the big hotels and national chains, and ask them the rate, you get some high priced quote followed by a long pause? Please understand they are only doing their job. Hotel reservation staff are trained to quote you a high rate, hoping, of course, you'll just say yes. (Hey, maybe I should start a new slogan for hotel rates, "Just Say No!" Think it might catch on?) After the first quote, this is when you need to go to work by asking the right questions.

"Do you have any specials?"

"Do you have weekend rates?"

"Do you have any senior citizen rates?"

"What about a family special?"

"Any promotions that include meals, like free breakfast?"

Hotel reservation agents are sometimes paid an incentive to book your reservation at a certain rate. If you ask the right questions, the rates usually start to drop. You must ask! Most hotels will not offer discounts until asked. Here are some of the hotel discount offers:

- Promotions and specials. These are often the best rates and are capacity controlled, meaning only a limited number of rooms are available at this rate. They usually have a name or "code word" identifying them. For example, Doubletree's *Dream Deals* and *Sweet Savers*, Hilton's *BounceBack Weekends*, Holiday Inn's *Weekender Special*, Radisson's *Bed and Breakfast Breakaway* promotion, etc. Even if you don't know the name of a specific promotion, ask what specials are being offered.
- Corporate rates. Usually a 10-20% discount.
- Preferred corporate rates. Usually a 20-40% discount. Specifically negotiated by a travel club, large agency, hotel consolidator, or individual corporate account.
- Low or off-season rates.
- Package rates. These may include breakfast, food credit, movies, late check-out, early check-in, resort activities, etc.
- Government rates.
- Convention rates.
- Shareholder rates. Some hotels will offer a special discount to shareholders.
- Discount rates when you fly a particular airline.
- Advance purchase rates.
- Frequent Flyer tie-in rates.

- Repeat or frequent guest rates.
- Less desirable rooms.
- Kids stay free.
- Same rate for up to 4, 5, or 6 persons sharing the same room.
- Senior citizen rates.
- Military rates.
- Discount cards, coupons, and books.
- Clergy rates.
- Long-term stay rates
- Association rates.
- AAA and other car/travel organization rates.
- Travel clubs.

How Fast Are You?
How long does it take to check in to a hotel, from the time you arrive at curbside to when your luggage arrives in your room? The envelope please. Answer: 12.1 minutes. The average time to check out is 7.9 minutes.[30]

Here are several ways to *Shop Smart* for discount hotel rates:

Hotel Consolidators. Several good companies have specialized in contracting hotel rooms at a savings of 20-70 percent off rack rates. In most cases, a hotel consolidator has a contract for a discounted rate "based upon availability." In some cases, hotel consolidators may have daily blocks of rooms and can therefore guarantee a room and rate on the spot. Here are some hotel consolidators (and there are many) that seem to do a fairly good job:

Hotel Plus specializes in Great Britain and Europe, but has a few properties in Asia, Africa, and the Middle East. Telephone: 800-235-0909.

Hotel Reservations Network. Telephone: 800-96HOTEL (800-964-6835). HRN has over 400 hotel properties on their discount program in major cities and resort centers of the United States, as well as properties in London and Paris.

Quikbook. Telephone: 800-789-9887. Books U.S. properties in 24 cities.

Room Exchange specializes primarily in upscale hotels in the United States, Mexico, the Caribbean, and several European and Asian cities. Telephone: 800-846-7000.

Travel Interlink. Telephone: 800-888-5898 or 818-986-8354. Offers discount rates in the South Pacific, Orient, Southeast Asia, and the Indian sub-continent.

Many of the Asian airline ticket consolidators also offer discount hotel rates in the Orient. As always, shop around.

Caution! Generally, hotel consolidators offer fairly good rates. I have used some hotel consolidators and saved a lot of money. Some of their rates, however, are no better than what is offered by the hotel, and in some cases, even higher. Shop and compare. It's your money!

Discount Hotel Books. There is a flood of discount hotel programs and directories. Almost all require a membership fee or purchase of their book. There are a few fairly good programs available, but most are a complete waste of time and money. Discount hotel books are also known as "Private Channel" sales.

Here are several discount hotel books:

America At 50%	$49.95	800-248-2783
Encore	$49.00	800-638-0930
Entertainment	$37.95	800-445-4137
ITC-50	$36.00	800-342-0558
Privilege Card	$74.95	800-236-9732
Quest	$99.00	800-638-9819

The problem with most discount directories, including those listed above, is that you must call each hotel yourself (and you never know if the discount rate is available until you call). Most discounts are only applicable if the hotel anticipates it will have less than an 80 percent occupancy rate. While the programs look, feel, and sound great, I have real doubts about the availability of rooms at a 50 percent discount rate. I did a recent test on two discount hotel books. I made 10 calls to randomly selected properties in each book and inquired about the discount listed in the book. Here are the results:

Book 1: All hotels contacted in this test were familiar with the details of the discount program. Not a single hotel could give me a room at that rate because they "anticipated" being more than 80 percent full.

Book 2: Of the 10 hotels contacted, eight were familiar with the discount hotel program listed in the book. Two hotels claimed no knowledge of the program, although both were listed in the book. Only one of the 10 hotels said they could confirm the discount rate from the book.

The **GEM** Consortium discount book, available through all GEM member travel agencies, is one of the better hotel books I've seen. The GEM rates are available, not just when the hotel is practically empty, but whenever a room is available. So, while the 50 percent discount book rates are only available if the hotel *anticipates* an occupancy rate of less than 80 percent, the GEM rates are available right down to the last room. In many cases, GEM offers the lowest rate. Most GEM rates, however, have been slightly higher than the 50 percent discount books. I go with GEM because I know the rate will always be available.

International Hotel Discount Books. Many of the discount hotel coupon books for U.S. travel also include some international locations. Listed below are several overseas discount programs. These books offer discounts at hotels in Europe and Canada. I have not found a discount program for travel to Asia that seems to offer any real benefits. I have found the best source of discount hotel rooms in Asia are airline ticket consolidators who sell travel to the Orient.

Carte Royal	$39.95	404-250-9950
Encore	$49.00	800-638-0930
Entertainment	$50.00	800-445-4137
Great American Traveler	$49.95	800-331-8867
ITC-50	$36.00	800-342-0558
Privilege Card	$74.95	800-236-9732
Solid Gold	$42.00 CAD	604-682-4296

The Paper Chase

A touchy issue! How do you rate the hotel toilet paper in different countries? Here's how 100 travel writers called it.[31] Do you agree?

United States	Very good
Japan	Good
Germany	Good
France	Average
Kenya	Average
Mexico	Average
Russia	Unbearable
China	Unbearable
India	Non-existent

Travel Clubs. A good travel club should have a hotel program, preferably one that offers a discount whenever the hotel has rooms available. If you are considering a travel club, ask them about the availability of their hotel discounts. Are the hotel discounts always available, or just sometimes? Chapter Four deals with travel clubs.

Negotiate your own. Do you want to have some fun? Don't feel stuck with the rack rate! It is an amount which is sometimes posted high just so it can discounted. There are two ways you can negotiate your own best hotel rate:

Call the hotel direct. Avoid chain or national reservation centers.

Those folks can't do much for you. Call the hotel direct. Ask for "reservations." The people on the front line are often empowered to make rate decisions to avoid losing a customer. Remember, just because you offer the hotel a lower rate, it doesn't mean that the hotel will accept it.

In person. Find out the asking room rate and then offer something less. I do this all the time. My reduced rate offers have never been received unkindly and often with a positive result. The manager is the best person to talk with as he/she is empowered to act.

I recently returned from a four-day trip to California with my children. We spent two days in Santa Cruz and two days in San Francisco. I arrived in Santa Cruz on the weekend (peak time) with no hotel reservations. I visited five different hotels in a matter of 20 minutes. In each case I negotiated with the manager. In four of the five cases, I was offered a special discounted rate based upon my counter offer to their rack rate. I finally settled on a good, medium priced hotel whose rack rate was $95. I offered $55. The owner said "no." He counter offered $70. We finally agreed upon a rate of $63.

I arrived at the Reno MGM Grand Hotel on a Wednesday evening around 10:30 p.m. I was told rooms were available and what the rate would be. I countered with an offer of half what the hotel was asking. I reasoned that it was mid-week, there were rooms available, and they probably would not rent all the rooms out tonight at this late hour. After some thought by the front desk manager, she accepted my offer.

Caution! I don't want to make this overly simplistic. I do not always get the price I want, but am usually successful in lowering my hotel rate. It may also sound like I usually travel without hotel reservations. Not true. I usually book my hotel in advance and always at a discount!

Out-of-town Newspapers. Get a copy of the Sunday newspaper from the city or area to which you are traveling. You can usually find the Sunday edition at a newsstand or bookstore. You can also find out-of-town newspapers at a public or university library. Locate the travel section. In most Sunday travel sections, local hotels advertise specials. Some are practically giving their rooms away. This is one of my best sources of discount hotel information.

Free Airport Hotel Magazines. These helpful guides are usually located in the luggage claim area, and they offer rock bottom prices. If you find a good offer, call the hotel to check availability before you cancel your existing room reservation. Usually these low rates are subject to availability and may not be applicable when the hotel is relatively full.

Hotel Script and Vouchers. Trading and bartering are common business practices today. Instead of paying for goods and services with cash, many hotels, particularly the large national chains, pay some bills with hotel credit called "script." The script or credit can be sold or traded by the recipient. There are barter companies that put parties together who want to trade their goods and services for another company's goods and services. Trading hotel script is common. If you buy script, buy it through your travel provider who is accountable to you if you run into any difficulties. You can buy a dollar's worth of hotel credit for a discounted amount, which can run from a small fraction on the dollar on up. Ask your travel provider about their experience in this area.

Hotel vouchers are different than script. Many hotel chains, especially overseas locations, sell pre-paid hotel vouchers. You can make reservations or just show up. The pre-paid vouchers, which have been bought at a discount, are exchanged as payment for your room. In most cases, unused vouchers can be returned and refunded. For example, *Flag International* is a chain of hotels throughout Australia and New Zealand. You can purchase a few vouchers or a book of pre-paid hotel vouchers. With your purchase you receive a directory of their locations. You can purchase vouchers for economy class, superior class, first class, and deluxe class hotels. Not only does it provide a discount, but it allows you to more accurately budget your trip since you know your hotel costs up front.

Special Affinity Offers. Many hotels offer special discounts to companies and organizations, and to their employees and family members. Check with any organization you have a membership in and ask if there are special hotel rates available.

Many hotels, particularly the chains, will offer repeat customer and recognition programs. Room upgrades, meals, and late check-out are typical benefits. It is always easier to keep a customer than to win a new one.

A common practice is to offer F&B (food and beverage) credits for guests staying and dining in the hotel, particularly on weekend stays. This can be part of a package deal, or negotiated by your company, travel club, or travel agency.

Many hotels, primarily in resort locations, will offer a discounted or free car rental for guests at their property. This is a very common practice in Hawaii and other "sun spots."

Senior Discounts. This may be the most common discount available. The age requirements vary, but can start as early as age 50. Most senior discounts run 10-15 percent, sometimes 25 percent and sometimes even more. There are several senior membership organizations, but their hotel discounts are not significantly greater than what is available through consolidators, travel clubs, or hotel discount books. Many senior discounts require an advance reservation. Remember the rule for discounts: Always ask!

Read more details on senior citizen discounts in Chapter Eight.

Life On The Road

An interesting, non-scientific survey was conducted by Novotel New York. The hotel housekeepers reported on men and women guests:

Who locked themselves out of their rooms more often?

Women; 70% were women and 30% were men.

Who found themselves in various stages of undress more often in the hotel corridors?

Sorry ladies, but you win again; 65% were women and 35% were men.

How many towels are used each day?

Men average two towels per day; women average four towels.

What do men leave behind most often?

Shoes and aftershave.

What do women leave behind most often?

Nightgowns.

Who leaves a cleaner room?

Men.

Corporate Rates. Many hotels offer a 10-25 percent discount for business travelers. In most cases, you can get a corporate rate just for the asking, regardless if you are on business or not. The corporate rate is a discount off of full or rack rate. Major corporations negotiate preferred corporate discounts of 30-50 percent off, sometimes even more, and often have special amenities, such as breakfast, early check-in, late check-out, upgrades, fax services, local telephone calls, and other perks thrown in free of charge as part of the package.

Ask your company travel planner if you can use the company's corporate rate on your next personal trip. Some hotels require a signed contract on file from your company to qualify for corporate rates.

Weekend Rates. At most hotels, weekend rates are available and offer substantial discounts, often with "gimmies" throw in, such as free meals and discounts on adjoining rooms. In some destinations, San Francisco, for example, the weekend rates may be higher than mid-week rates. **Seasonal rates**, which include weekend rates, are hotel rates adjusted for peak and off-peak periods. If you want to go when everyone else wants to, you'll pay for the privilege!

Frequent Flyer Mileage. Ask if your hotel offers airline Frequent Flyer Mileage. Most independent and small hotels don't, but always ask. Most, but not all, national chains do. You will not automatically receive your mileage credit. Remember, mileage is an expense to the hotel. You must ask for it to receive it.

Little Known Accommodations. There is a wide variety of alternate lodging accommodations available. They may not meet the needs of everyone, but for the budget conscious and adventurous traveler, it may fit the bill. (Pun intended!)

Universities and Colleges. Many universities rent their dorms while school is out of session and provide both excellent value and an ideal location. Colleges and universities are usually well located and offer a wide variety of activities both on and off campus. In most cases, you have access to school facilities, such as swimming pools, gymnasiums, library, tennis courts, etc. One of the best low cost accommodation guides, which includes an extensive list of colleges and university dorms, is *Budget Lodging Guide*, B&J Publications. Telephone: 800-525-6633. The book includes over 4,000 listings for college and university dorms, hostels, YMCA accommodations, B&B, home sharing, and other economy stays. The guide includes approximately 650 college dorms available for guests. The book also lists over 100 international choices, from a twin-bed $25 room in Vienna, to a $300-a-week apartment at the University of Siena in Tuscany, Italy.

For information on universities in the United Kingdom, contact British Universities Accommodation Consortium, Box 966-ATW, University Park, Nottingham NG7 2RD, England. Telephone: (011) (44) 115-950-45-71.

Youth Hostels. It is a misconception to think that only young backpackers can or do stay in youth hostels. Youth hostels usually offer both shared, family, and private accommodations. All provide firsthand knowledge of the local color and sights to be seen. The quality of rooms and facilities vary from location to location. Guide books can be a good source of individual hostel information. Reservations are recommended. Two good sources of hostel information are: Hostelling International, telephone: 202-783-4943; and International Youth Hostel Federation, which represents almost 5,000 hostels in 77 countries, telephone: 202-783-6161.

My family and I stayed in several youth hostels on a recent trip to Australia and New Zealand and found them to be clean, basic, well located, and inexpensive.

Europe stays. An excellent source of hotel information in western Europe can be found at train stations. Although little used in this country, train travel is the *modus operandi* for Europeans. At large city train stations, a staffed hotel information and reservation office will assist you with your lodging needs. You tell them how much you want to spend and if you have a preferred location. They will recommend various properties, call the hotel, and even make a reservation for you. There is a nominal charge for this service. At the train station in smaller cities and villages, there is usually a posted list of lodging accommodations and rates. Many of these hotel boards have a telephone connection direct to the hotel for reservations and directions.

Room space can be tight in peak season, but is rarely a problem during off-peak times. I have used these services for years and not only saved a lot of money, but I like the flexibility of not having pre-paid or deposited reservations with cancellation penalties.

Last December, my wife, Cathy, and I flew to Germany for a week. I love Germany, especially at Christmas time. We spent a few days in Nürnberg at the *Christkindl* market, a century old Christmas celebration. Driving from Munich through the Bavarian Alps to Berchtesgaden, Mittenwald, Garmisch, and Oberammergau during winter is spectacular!

We arrived by car in Oberammergau. This is the home of the *Passionspiel*, or Passion Play (an eight hour dramatization of the last week or Passion Week of Christ, which has been performed by the town's citizens every ten years continuously since 1634 to honor a vow taken by the village after they were spared from the devastating plague of 1633).

We had no reservations as we did not know from one night to the next where we would find ourselves. So what did we do? Two possibilities. We could go to the train station, and/or to the local tourist office. I saw a sign for visitor's information and pulled in. A helpful agent in the tourist office made several hotel, *pension*, and *gasthäuser* recommendations. She called a hotel, made a reservation for us, and gave us directions.

Traveling in the off-season, I only made advance reservations for our first two nights in Nürnberg, which is usually crowded during the *Christkindl* market. Everywhere else we went, we "winged" it. No problems.

P.S., if you're looking for rooms in Germany, look for a *Zimmer Frei* ("rooms for rent") sign in the window.

P.P.S. It has been said that Disneyland's Cinderella castle was patterned after the Bavarian *Neuschwanstein* castle near Füssen. I think it was!

Bed and Breakfast. These accommodations vary from simple and basic to deluxe. Some may actually be a spare or side room at a private home, others may be an inn or home which is exclusively a B&B. I've enjoyed B&B stays all over the world. I save a lot of money and enjoy meeting new people. If I'm overseas, I can experience a new culture in ways I never could have in a large hotel.

A good source of B&B locations are tourist bureaus. B&B stays are often associated with Europe. Most national tourist offices will provide B&B lists or recommend books that identify and rate B&B lodgings. Visit the travel section of your favorite bookstore. There should be several books on B&B accommodations to wherever you may be traveling.

For B&B reservations in the United States, British Columbia, Europe, and the South Pacific, contact Bed & Breakfast Reservation Services Worldwide; telephone: 504-296-7470.

For B&B stays in Britain, call Hometours International; telephone: 800-367-4668 or 615-588-8722. The British Tourist Authority also provides B&B information for Great Britain; telephone: 800-462-2748 or 212-986-2200. For other overseas B&B, contact the tourist board for that country.

Here are some questions you should ask if you are considering a B&B or home stay:

"What is the daily rate?"

"Does that includce all taxes and charges?"

"Is there a separate outside entrance?"

"Is there a private or shared bathroom?"

"Does the rate include a shower and/or bath?" Some B&Bs charge extra for taking a bath rather than a shower.

"Can guests visit me?"

"Is the room and/or home a smoking or non-smoking environment?"

"Are children welcome? What about pets in the house or with other guests?"

"Can I lock my door?"

"What time is breakfast served?" If you have any special dietary restrictions, ask if you can be accommodated.

"Do you accept credit cards, or cash only?"

"Are you located near shops and public transportation? If yes, how far?"

If a deposit is required, "What are your cancellation policies?"

"Are you a member of a travel or lodging organization?"

It is always advisable, although not always possible, to get this information in writing.

For your reference, a list of tourist boards and offices is included in Appendix 3. You can find almost any foreign tourist office by calling telephone information directory assistance for New York City or Los Angeles. Most foreign tourist organizations staff offices in one or both of these cities.

Caution Alert: The latest surprise many hotels are trying to impose on travelers are early check-out penalties. For example, if you book for three nights, but check-out after two, some hotels may attempt to charge you an early cancellation penalty. The hotels' rationale is that your early departure eliminates any chance of re-selling that room. I say, "Bunk!"

Best Advice: Book early and shop around. Even if you're not sure of your plans, book your hotel room now and you stand the best chance of getting a discount. If your plans change, you can always cancel your reservation, but if you do go, you'll probably pay less than the guy in the next room. That's how to **Shop Smart!**

Chapter 7
Car Rentals
And How Not To Crash!

Renting a car and getting the best price can drive you nuts! Rates are not constant. Car rates change daily depending upon how many cars are available. If a rental car company suddenly finds itself with too many unrented cars, down come the rates. If supply is tight and demand high, up go the rates.

Don't assume that all car rental rates are the same. In the same city, the rate for renting the same make and model of car, but from different car companies, can vary a few dollars to more than double the price. Here are the best strategies for driving your rental car rate to the bottom:

Corporate Rates. Car rental rates are discounted to corporations. Ask what the "corporate rate" is. Although originally intended for the business traveler, just for asking, some car rental companies now require a signed agreement between the car company and a particular corporation. Ask your company's travel planner to book you a car at the corporate rate. Some travel clubs and travel agencies have a "generic" corporate ID number that anyone, for business or vacation travel, can use. Always ask!

Association Rates. Very similar to corporate rates. Various associations and organizations negotiate discounts for car rentals. What organizations, credit unions, and for service groups are you a member of? Always ask!

Travel Clubs. A good travel club will have a negotiated discount rate and upgrade options for its members.

Airline Passenger Rates. Many car rental companies offer discounts if you fly a particular airline. Members of airline frequent flyer programs also receive discounts. Remember, you never get these or other discounts unless you ask!

Senior Rates. Most car rental companies will offer a 5-10 percent discount to senior citizens. If the car company does not have their own senior citizen rate, chances are they have an AARP rate, which usually amounts to the same discounts. At present, Alamo, Avis, Budget, Dollar, Enterprise, Hertz, National, Payless, and Thrifty offer a senior citizen and/or AARP rate.

Upgrades. Do you really want a full-size car, but want to pay an economy rate? Car upgrades, i.e., paying for one category of car, but driving out in a larger car, is so common place; we don't even raise our eyebrows to it anymore! Your travel agent should be offering you upgrade and savings discount coupons every time you book. You shouldn't have to ask. Some upgrade offers require a minimum rental period. Others do not.

When I arrive at the counter to pick up my rental car, I am usually asked by the agent if I would like to pay an increased amount and upgrade to a larger car. On more than one occasion, I have received the larger car after I have declined the upgrade. Why? The car size that I reserved is not available and consequently I am given a larger car at no charge. Surprisingly, if I am traveling alone, I really prefer the smaller car. It's easy to park and uses less gas.

Sunday Newspaper Travel Section. Car rental deals, with or without airfare, are frequently listed in the travel section of your Sunday newspaper. Remember to check the newspaper travel sections of the cities you will be visiting. Some of the best deals are local and regional. You can find out-of-town newspapers at many bookstores, libraries, and on the Internet.

One-way Rentals. Typically, one-way rentals carry stiff "drop-off" charges. From time to time, some rental car companies will offer great rates to help them move their cars from one location to another. For example, toward the end of the summer season, several car rental companies often find a surplus of cars and vans in the Los Angeles area and a shortage in the San Francisco area. (It seems more people like to drive south than north between the cities.) There is no schedule or guarantee, but I have seen some very, very low rates with no drop-off charges attached for one-way northbound rentals.

As this book goes to press, National is offering a rate of $9.95 a day rate, up to 14 days, for rentals from any one of 61 locations in the Eastern United States to Florida. The same price applies to a mid-size car, full-size car, or minivan. Do you think National needs to get cars to Florida for winter rentals? Yep!

These types of deals come and go with little notice. It's more a matter of luck (and knowing about it) than advance planning. Advise your travel agent that you are interested in discounted one-way rentals. Like most travel deals, you need an information source that will continuously keep you informed.

Check the classified section of your newspaper. Companies and individuals regularly advertise for people to drive their cars from one city or state to another. Usually, you are responsible for the gasoline.

Overlooking Rio de Janiero, Brazil. (*above*) A koala is a marsupial, not a bear. Sydney, Australia. (*right*) Walking to the Hermitage Museum in St. Petersburg, Russia. (*below*)

Hans Christian Andersen country in Copenhagen, Denmark. The city dates to 1167. (*above*) Kinkaku-ji Temple or Temple of the Golden Pavilion dates to 1397. Kyoto, Japan. (*below*)

Group travel is fun and can save a lot of money! U.S.A. national champion Highland Rugby (which I coach) on tour in Sydney, Australia. Yes, we won all our matches in Aussie! (*above*)
Deep sea fishing in Mazatlan, Mexico. (*left*)

London, one of the greatest cities in the world, with Parliament in the background.
(*above*)
The dome of the Rock sacred to Moslems, Jews, and Christians.
Jerusalem, Israel.
(*right*)

One of the joys of family travel is making new friends!
(*left*)

Bungy jumping 17 stories down to the Waikato River in
Taupo, New Zealand. (*above*) Cruising is my favorite hol-
iday. Cathy and I sailing aboard the *Crystal Harmony* in
Europe. (*below*)

I lived with Aborigines deep in the Australian Outback. Lunch was always an adventure! (*above left*) Just another day in paradise - Jamaica! (*above right*) Vava'u Beach, Samoa. Nu'utele Island in the distance. (*below*)

Alaska. America's last frontier. (*above*) The Sphinx and pyramids of ancient Egypt. (*below*)

As a certified scuba diver, I have enjoyed diving all over the world. (*right*)

Whitewater rafting the Kaituna River, New Zealand. (*left*)

The Mahatma Gandhi Shrine. New Delhi, India. (*right*)

Counter Shopping. When you arrive at your destination and are waiting for your luggage to arrive, shop the car rental counters. Ask other car rental companies what their best rate is. Matching your rate isn't good enough, they need to beat it and not by a few pennies. If you do find a better rate, cancel your other reservation. Not only is it the right thing to do, but "no shows" drive up the rental rate for everyone.

Is CDW a good deal? That depends on what you are buying it for. Collision Damage Waiver, erroneously called insurance (which it is not), is a waiver of liability if your rental car is damaged. The price of CDW coverage is high and may run anywhere from $8 to $13 a day for automobiles, and even more for vans or trucks.

Is it worth it? Well, if you simply want coverage, the answer is "no." CDW provides peace of mind. If you are in an accident, unless you are involved in some illegal or prohibited activity (like four-wheeling with your rented Buick!), you can simply walk away from liability to the rental car company.

Let There Be Light!
Avis reports that drivers who keep their headlights on during the day have 69% fewer accidents than drivers who drive without the lights on.

What about coverage provided by my credit card? Some credit cards provide liability coverage if you decline the rental car company's CDW option and pay for the rental with that card. Check with your credit card company to determine exactly what is covered and what is not. Read the fine print. Some types and makes of vehicles, typically specialty cars—four-wheel drive vehicles and vans—may be excluded from credit card coverage.

Is your coverage primary or secondary? Are there deductibles? What is excluded from coverage? What and who is included?

If you are involved in an accident or your rental car is damaged, regardless of who is actually responsible for the damage, you are liable to the rental car company. If you have purchased their CDW, you can walk away because the CDW releases you from damage liability to the rental car, assuming you have not violated any of the terms of your rental agreement.

Suppose you decline the CDW because you have coverage through your credit card and you are involved in an accident. Suppose the other car and driver are 100 percent at fault. What happens? You are liable to the rental car company for the damage. You may have legal recourse to pursue the guilty party, but that is strictly between you and the other driver. The car rental company is not a party to the problem, other than they own the damaged car. You can't say, "Well, it was his fault, he got cited by the police, so go after him." Nope, can't do it. You rented the car, and you are responsible to the rental company.

Here's a big surprise: with most rental car agreements, you are not only responsible for the repair of damages to the car, but are responsible for the lost rental revenue while the car is being repaired. Translation: You are stuck for the monies the rental car company **would** have received if that car had been available for rental. This is called **Lost Revenue Liability.** This alone could amount to thousands of dollars. Now, you may have legal recourse with the other party, but that's between you and the other person. CDW waives your Lost Revenue Liability.

Ask yourself these questions:

- Do I have any coverage through third parties, viz., credit cards, organizations, personal insurance, etc? Usually credit card coverage includes only collison damage, not liability coverage.
- If yes, *exactly* what is covered. Read the boring pamphlet details.
- Does my own insurance cover Lost Revenue Liability?
- Are any vehicle types excluded? This may often include luxury cars, specialty cars, trucks, RVs, and four-wheel drive vehicles
- Is PAI covered (Personal Accident Insurance)?
- Is PEC covered (Personal Effects Coverage)?
- Is the CDW primary or secondary coverage? Secondary coverage pays for whatever your primary insurance coverage does not cover.
- Is there a deductible? What is the amount? What does it include and exclude?
- Is damage to the other car covered in my CDW?

What about coverage provided by my personal automobile insurance company? Ask yourself the same questions as those listed with credit card coverage. Exactly what is included and excluded. What is the extent of your coverage. Does your personal car insurance cover Lost Reveneue Liability?

International Rentals. Renting and driving in another country is different in many ways, sometimes even the side of the road you drive on! Here is a checklist to remember when you are planning to drive overseas:

- You can often reduce your cost by pre-paying the rental in this country. An advantage is that you know exactly what the cost is because you have paid in U.S. dollars.
- Is there a refund for early return?
- Unlimited kilometers. Is there any mileage charge?
- Car features: automatic or shift transmission, air conditioning, trunk

size, how many passengers will the automobile comfortably sit, number of seat belts, etc.

- Country driving restrictions. Are there any areas I am not allowed to drive in? Many European companies do not allow cars rented in Western Europe to be taken into Eastern Europe. (Too many disappearing cars, especially Mercedes!) Also, cars are usually not allowed to be taken from Great Britain to the continent and vice versa.
- Is Value Added Tax (V.A.T.) included in the rate or is it additional? V.A.T. can run as high as 23%.
- If you are paying overseas, what form of payment must be provided? Which, if any, credit cards are accepted.
- Get a list of all other rental locations. Will other locations help if the car breaks down or if you are involved in an accident?
- Inspect the vehicle thoroughly. If there is any damage whatsoever, insist it be noted on the rental agreement or you may be held liable.
- Don't sign anything you can't read. Too many people get burned signing rental agreements in a foreign language and then finding big surprises!
- Make sure everything operates properly before you leave the rental location.
- Is an International Driver's License required? AAA can help you with this. In some countries, you are required to obtain a visitor's driving permit from the local authorities after you arrive. In most countries, your home state driver's license is sufficient. Do not assume that because your own driver's license is accepted that there is nothing else you need to do. In Western Samoa, for example, you are not required to get a local driving permit from the Samoan government, but it's a good idea. You can rent a car and drive in Samoa with your U.S.A. license. If you are involved in an accident, however, the police will not fill out an official report unless you have a local driving permit (available at the police station for $10 WST— about $4 USD). Even if you have purchased CDW on your rental in Samoa, it does not take effect unless you have a police report, and you cannot get a police report without a local driving permit. There are other countries who have similar regulations. Always check the local regulations.

I have found good rates and reliable reservations with Alamo (800-GO-ALAMO or 800-462-5266), Kemwel (800-678-0678), and Auto Europe (800-223-5555). You may think of Alamo as just an American vacation car rental company, but think again! Alamo has 114 European locations.

There are many good rental car companies. My personal favorite for the United States and Europe is **Alamo Rent A Car.** Not only do I find consistently good rates and friendly service, but Alamo has been aggressive in distributing discount and upgrade coupons. There are several worthwhile Alamo programs you may want to consider:

- *True Blue Awards.* A unique customer recognition and award program. In addition to earning frequent flyer mileage credit, you earn Alamo *True Blue* points that can be redeemed for free travel.
- *Quicksilver.* After enrollment, you receive a special card that is inserted into a kiosk at Alamo. With your advance reservation, your contract is printed in less than 60 seconds. (My experience has been a 30 second average.) You are told where the car is and the keys are already in the car.
- *All-Inclusive Rates.* One rate, everything is included: car, unlimited miles, CDW, children seats, ski racks if needed, tax, and the list goes on and on. Excellent value!
- *Frequent Flyer Miles.* One of the more comprehensive airline frequent flyer award programs.

☞ Here's *really* good advice. Always write down your car rental confirmation number and rate. More than once I have arrived at a rental counter only to find an agent unable to find my reservation. I produce my confirmation number and bingo, suddenly my car appears. I've also been questioned by the rental agent about my rate. If you were quoted a particular rate, hold them to it!

☞ More *really* good advice. On a few occasions, I have arrived to pick-up my car and found the rental company unable to provide a car. There are two probable reasons for this. First, the car rental company has "oversold" their inventory. As do airlines, hotels, and cruise lines, car rental companies also take more reservations than they have available cars. Their yield management department predicts how many cancellations and no-shows they will have. Sometimes the "bean counters" are wrong. Second, a renter does not return his vehicle promised, and this creates a shortage of cars.

What do you do? Keep your cool. The poor agent behind the desk didn't do this to you. Ask when a car will be ready. Press the agent for his/her "guarantee" that the next available car will go to you! If your wait is prolonged, ask for a complimentary upgrade, free day, or other "*feel good*" concessions. If you are on a tight schedule, some car rental companies will pay your cab fare to your meeting or appointment (this happened to me in San Diego) and will bring the car to your hotel. If you wish to press the issue further, write down the names of who you talked with at the counter, your confirmation number, and facts pertinent to your case. Type a letter to the

Consumer Relations department of the rental car company. Usually you will get a form letter back and sometimes a coupon for future free days and/or other consideration.

Chapter 8
Senior Citizen Discounts
Golden Rates In The Golden Years

What is a "Senior Citizen?" Depending on who you talk to, it is someone who is age 50, 55, 60, 62, or 65 or older! Sometimes when you say "Senior Citizen," you get a vision of one foot in the grave and one foot out. Not so! (I'm not there yet, but 50, 55, 60, 62, or 65 years does not sound too old to me!) Actually, this age group is one of the most active traveling groups. Most have grown families, discretionary time, and some discretionary income. Remember, traveling doesn't have to be expensive....not when you know how to *Shop Smart* for senior discounts.

Here are a few general guidelines for senior discount travel (don't you think "senior discount travel" sounds better than "senior citizen travel?"):

- Always ask. Almost every airline, cruise line, hotel, and car rental company provides senior discount rates. These discounts are almost never offered up front, you have to ask for them. The worst that can happen is that you are told "no," and then you're no worse off than if you had never asked. Most of the time you will receive some discount.
- Ask for your discount when you make your reservation.
- Compare your senior discount rate with other discount rates. You will almost always receive a senior discount, but often times other discounts and special promotions will save you more.
- Some discounts are restricted to various times or days of the week. Others are seasonal.
- Always carry proof of age with you. You may be asked for it.
- Join one of the senior citizen organizations. They often provide very good discounts.

Consider these:

American Association of Retired Persons (AARP)
601 "E" Street NW
Washington, D.C. 20049
Telephone: 202-434-2277

AARP is open to all persons age 50 years or older, retired or not. Annual membership fee is $8 per household. Membership benefits include discounts on: hotels, resorts, and auto rentals; motor club for trip planning; auto and homeowner's insurance; supplemental health insurance; bi-monthly magazine; 4,000+ local chapters with a variety of activities; volunteer programs; and so on.

Canadian Association of Retired Persons (CARP)
27 Queen Street
Suite 1304
Toronto, Ontario M5C 2M6
Canada
Telephone: 416-363-8748

CARP is open to all Canadians who are 50 years of age or older, retired or not. Dues are $10 CAD annually, or $25 CAD for three years. Provides similar programs and benefits as AARP.

There are many other associations, including:

Catholic Golden Age	800-233-4697
Mature Outlook (Sears)	800-336-6330
National Council of	
Senior Citizens	800-333-7212
	202-347-8800
National Association for Retired	
Credit Union People	608-232-6070
National Association of Retired	
Federal Employees	800-627-3394
	202-234-0832
Older Women's League	800-825-3695
	202-783-6686
National Alliance of	
Senior Citizens	202-986-0117
The Retired Officers Association	800-245-8762
	703-549-2311

Of all the groups, the travel discounts available through AARP seem to offer the best deals.

AIRLINE DISCOUNTS. It is unusual not to receive a senior discount on your airline ticket. Typically, you will receive a 10 percent discount off an applicable fare. Sometimes it can be much more. Canadian Airlines International offers a program called 60/60, which gives passengers ages 60+ and their traveling companions a 60 percent discount off full-fare tickets. If you are buying at the last minute, this 60 percent discount will help. If you have enough time to buy an advance purchase ticket, compare the cost. You will probably be entitled to a 10 percent discount off the advance purchase ticket. In most cases, this would give a lower fare than a 60 percent discount off full-fare.

Senior Citizen Airline Coupon Books: This is one of the best, yet least known discount programs. You buy a book of blank air travel tickets, each with your name written on it, but not your destination. The tickets are all priced the same regardless of where you are going, although Hawaii, Alaska, and international travel may require more than one ticket coupon. For example, TWA sells a book of four ticket coupons for only $548. That's $137 per coupon. One coupon is required for a one-way trip, and two coupons are required for a round trip. With TWA's *Senior Travel Pack,* you can fly anywhere in the 48 states, Jamaica, Mexico, San Juan, Santo Domingo, and Toronto for only one coupon each way, or $274 round trip. At present, the following airlines offer senior coupon books: America West, American, Continental, Delta, Kiwi, Northwest, Southwest, TWA, United, and USAir. The terms, conditions, rules, and prices vary from airline to airline.

Senior Citizen Discount Airline Coupon Books

Airline	Cost per book and per coupon	Terms and Conditions
America West *Senior Savers* 800-235-9292	4 coupons: $495 ($124) 8 coupons: $920 ($115)	Travel within 48 states; 14-day AR; travel noon Monday to noon Thursday, all day Saturday; some blackout dates.
American *Senior TrAAveler* 800-237-7981	4 coupons: $596 ($149)	Travel within 48 states, to Puerto Rico and the U.S. Virgin Islands; 14-day AR, valid all days; no blackout dates; 2 coupons each way to Hawaii.

Continental *Freedom Trips* 800-248-8996	4 coupons: $579 ($145) 8 coupons: $999 ($125)	Travel within 48 states, to Montreal, Toronto, Mexico and the Caribbean; valid all days; 14-day AR; some blackout dates; 2 coupons each way to Alaska and Hawaii.
Delta *Senior Citizen Booklet* 800-221-1212	4 coupons: $596 ($149)	Travel within 48 states and to San Juan; 14-day AR; valid all days; no blackout dates; 2 coupons each way to Alaska, Hawaii, and St. Thomas.
Kiwi Int'l[32] *Senior Bonus Pack* 800-538-5494	6 coupons: $600 ($100)	Travel within 48 states; 7-day AR; valid all days; no blackout dates.
Northwest *Senior Best* 800-225-2525	4 coupons: $596 ($149)	Travel within 48 states and to Canada; 14-day AR; no blackout dates; 2 coupons each way to Alaska and Hawaii.
Southwest *Senior Fares* 800-435-9792	$34 to $129 per ticket	Travel within 48 states; no AR; valid all days; no blackout dates; fully refundable.
TWA *Senior Travel Pack* 800-221-2000	4 coupons: $ 548 ($137) Companion: $ 648 ($162) 8 coupons: $1,032 ($129) Companion: $1,132 ($142)	Travel within 48 states and to Jamaica, Mexico, San Juan, Santo Domingo, and Toronto;14-day AR; valid all days; no blackout dates; 2 coupons each way to Hawaii; includes a 20% discount coupon to Europe.

United *Silver Travel Pac* 800-633-6563	4 coupons: $596 ($149)	Travel within 48 states, to Canada and San Juan; 14-day AR; valid all days; no blackout dates except for Hawaii; 2 coupons each way to Alaska and Hawaii, except Seattle to Anchorage or Fairbanks.
USAir *Golden Opportunities* 800-428-4322	4 coupons: $596 ($149)	Travel within 48 states and to Canada, Mexico, San Juan and St. Thomas; 14-day AR;valid all days; no blackout dates.

✈ "48 states" means travel on the airline's route system within the 48 contiguous states.

✈ "AR" means advance reservation requirement. An AR is required by most carriers to receive a confirmed seat, but you can usually stand-by without reservations.

✈ "Valid all days" means there is no restriction as to travel on a particular day of the week.

✈ If you are planning a trip to Hawaii, check the cost of an excursion fare, less your senior discount, split fare, tour fare, and a consolidator ticket with the cost of four senior coupons (two coupons each way). In most cases, senior coupons are not a good value for travel to Hawaii. The same is true for travel to Alaska and the Caribbean where two coupons are required each way for travel. *Shop Smart!*

Continental Airlines Senior Freedom Passport: This is a great offer for travelers 62 years and older. Pay a single price and fly every week during the length of your Freedom Passport. You can buy four and 12-month "passports." Passes are available for both Coach and First Class for domestic and international travel. The *Global Passport* allows domestic travel plus one round-trip to Hawaii, Alaska, and Central America and two round-trips to Europe, Mexico, and the Caribbean. A traveling companion of any age may purchase a pass. The passport allows you to take a flight every week. You select a home city which cannot be changed. You can fly a maximum of three times to the same destination. There are some holiday blackout dates. Generally, domestic travel is valid noon Monday through noon Thursday, and anytime Saturday. You must stay over a Sunday night. You can stay a long time, or as little as two days. Reservations may be made no earlier than seven days in advance. For international travel, you may travel Monday through Thursday and Saturday. International reservations may be made no earlier than 30 days in advance.

Why do I say this is one of the best travel bargains around? Consider this: suppose you bought a four-month domestic Coach Passport. Your cost is $999. This entitles you to travel as much or as little as you wish, not to exceed once a week. Suppose you took eight round-trips on a four-month domestic passport. Your round-trip cost would be only $125 per trip! (That's only $62.50 each way, and you can fly anywhere in Continental's domestic 48 state route system.) Okay, you can't go every week, so you take six round-trips in a four month period. Now your round-trip cost is $167. Suppose you want to live it up and buy a 12-month domestic First Class passport. You don't fly every week. You take, say, 20 round-trips during the year....all up front in First Class. Your round-trip cost per trip is only....are you ready for this...$175 in First Class!

Continental Airlines Freedom Passport

4-month Domestic Coach Passport	$ 999
12-month Domestic Coach Passport	$1,999
12-month Domestic First Class Passport	$3,499
12-month Coach Global Passport	$4,499
12-month First Class Global Passport	$6,999

Delta Air Lines' Senior Select Savings Plus. This can reduce airfares by 38-50 percent for seniors ages 62 and older. Delta has established their own senior discount travel club. Select Plus annual membership is $40 single, $65 for a couple, and $70 for up to four persons (seniors and grandchildren ages 2-12). You can change the person included in the four person plan for $25 per name change. Delta has divided the country into seven zones. Discount fares are offered for travel within your zone and between zones. Select Plus travel dates are November 18, 1996 through April 1, 1998. Enrollment is limited and is scheduled to close April 1, 1997 or when the program limit is reached. To enroll, call Delta at 800-325-3750.

Discounts on U.S. Airlines. I hesitate to list airfares or discounts anywhere in this book because prices change more often than do high school sweethearts! But here goes. It will give you a good idea of what is available. Always check and compare.

Senior Discounts on U.S. Airlines

Airline	Senior Age	Discount
Air South	60 years	Discount off seven-day advance purchase fare; discount amount varies according to destination.
Alaska	62 years	10% off
American West	62 years	10% off regular coach fares
American	62 years	10% off
Continental	62 years	10% off
Delta	62 years	10% off "Young At Heart" fares
Delta Shuttle	62 years	Up to 50% off regular fares Restricted hours
Hawaiian	60 years	10% on certain fares to Hawaii and inter-island travel
Lone Star	62 years	10% off
Midwest Express	62 years	10% off
Northwest	62 years	10% off
Reno Air	62 years	10% off
Southwest	65 years	Senior Fares; vary according to city pairs.
TWA	62 years	10% off
United	62 years	10% off
USAir	62 years	10% off
USAir Shuttle	62 years	50% off shuttle flights between New York City, Boston, and Washington, D.C., restricted hours

✈ Sometimes special promotional fares and fare war "matching" fares are excluded.

✈ Delta Shuttle: You may travel Monday - Thursday between 10:30 a.m. and 2:30 p.m.; 7:30 p.m. and 9:30 p.m.; and all day Saturday and Sunday.

✈ **Kids Fly Free On the Delta Shuttle.** Children ages 2 to 12 fly free on the hourly Delta Shuttle between New York City, Boston, and Washington, D.C. One child is allowed with one adult purchasing the $54 one-way fare. You can fly anytime Saturday or on Sunday until 11:30 a.m. Tickets must be purchased at least three days in advance. Currently, there is no expiration date.

✈ USAir Shuttle: You may travel Monday - Friday 10:00 a.m. to 2:00 p.m.; 7:00 p.m. to midnight; all day Saturday and Sunday.

Discounts on International Airlines. Many international airlines offer senior discounts, including Air Canada, Canadian International, Aerolineas Argentinas, Aerolitoral, Aeromexico, Air France, Air Inter, Alitalia, British Airways, NWIA, El Al, Finnair, Iberia, KLM Royal Dutch Airlines, Lufthansa, Mexicana, Sabena Belgian, SAS, Swissair, and TAP Air Portugal. Most discounts are 10 percent, some a little higher.

Always compare your senior discount fare to prices available through a consolidator. In most cases, a consolidator ticket will cost less than a published fare less the senior discount.

Senior Rental Car Discounts

Car Rental	Senior Age	Discount
Advantage	AARP	10% off
Alamo	50 years	5-10% off
Avis	AARP, CARP, and Mature Outlook	5-10% off
Budget	AARP, Mature Outlook & CARP	5% off in the United States 10% off in Canada
Dollar	65 years	5% off
Enterprise	AARP	10% off
Hertz	AARP, Y.E.S., Mature Outlook, NARFE, & ROA.	5-10% off
	United Silver Wings	10% off
National	AARP, CARP, & Mature Outlook	10% off
Thrifty	55 years	10% off
Value	AARP	5% off

RENTAL CARS. Almost every car rental company offers some form of senior discount. It may be their own rate or a special AARP rate. As with airfares, compare the rate after your senior discount with other special discount rates. Sometimes your senior discount is not applicable to low promotional rates.

SENIOR HOTEL DISCOUNTS. Hotels routinely offer a senior discount, but the discounts are rarely comparable with rates from consolidators. Senior discounts are best used for economy and mid-priced accommodations. Senior discounts are usually 5-15 percent off the regular or "rack" rate, sometimes as much as 25-50 percent off. If the hotel has a restaurant, ask about senior meal discounts. Specially priced meals and 10-20 percent off the regular menu are typical. Some of the hotels charge a membership fee to participate in their senior program.

Alaska Wildland Adventures offers programs for the 50+ age crowd who want to see Alaska on a relaxed pace. Trips are normally seven to nine days. If you belong to a senior organization, you get a $50 discount. Telephone: 800-334-8730.

Creative Adventure Club operates two week "soft" adventure trips. A relaxed pace and itinerary allows travelers to get a close look and understanding of the people and culture visited. You may travel with a senior group or have FIT arrangements made for you. Telephone: 800-544-5088.

Elderhostel offers a wide variety of lodging, activities, and even meal options. Some programs are designed for guests with special interests. Elderhostel operates in the United States, Canada, and Europe. Telephone 617-426-7788. In Canada, telephone: 613-530-2222.

FamilyHostel takes families (parents, children, grandparents, etc.) on 10-day and two-week summer trips overseas when the kids are out of school. Trips are well planned and combine fun activities with cultural and education opportunities. Telephone: 800-733-9753.

Grandparents and Grandchildren Camps are offered by the College of the Tehachapis in California. Six-day camp sessions for grandparents and their grandchildren are organized at very affordable prices. Telephone: 800-224-8115 or 805-823-8115.

Hostelling International-American Youth Hostels. Remember hostels are not just for the young. HI-AYH coordinates 5,000 hostels in 70 countries. You can travel on your own or join a tour program. Youth and senior tours are offered. Telephone: 800-444-6111 or 202-783-6161.

Hostelling International - Canada. HI-C represents 80 hostels throughout Canada. Telephone 613-237-7884.

Overseas Adventure Club offers "soft" adventure programs worldwide designed for the 50+ year old group. Tours to Central America, South America, Europe, and Egypt are offered. Telephone: 800-353-6262 or 617-876-0533.

NATIONAL PARKS. The "Golden Age Passport" entitles anyone age 62 or over a lifetime pass for free admission to the U.S. national parks, forests, refuges, and monuments. Anyone accompanying you gets in free, too—provided you are traveling in a non-commercial vehicle. You also receive up to a 50 percent discount on camping, boat marinas, parking, and cave tours.

The pass can only be obtained in person at any National Park

System office where admission fees are charged or any office of the National Park Service, U.S. Forest Service, the Fish and Wildlife Service, or the Bureau of Land Management. Proof of age is required. The cost is $10.

SENIOR RAIL DISCOUNTS. Here we go again. More discounts! Most trains will offer a senior discount, although some are seasonal. Train discounts are generally available on both individual tickets and rail passes.

Senior Rail Discounts

North America

Rail Company	Senior Age	Discount or Program
Amtrak *800-872-7245*	62 years	15% off
Alaska Railroad *800-544-0552*	65 years	50% off weekend fares late September to mid-May
Via Rail Canada *800-561-3949*	60 years	10% off all year 40% off-peak travel

Europe: Rail

Company/Country	Senior Age	Discount or Program
Eurailpass *See your travel club or travel agent*	N/A	No senior discount
Europass *See your travel club or travel agent*	N/A	No senior discount
Austria Federal Rail *212-944-6880*	Women 60 yrs + Men 65 yrs +	50% 50%
Belgium *212-758-8130*	60 years	Golden Railpasses
France National Rail *212-838-7800 (Information only)*	60 years +	50% off, restricted hours 30% off intra-Europe
Great Britain *USA: 800-677-8585* *Canada: 800-387-7245*	60 years +	Old Age Pensioners rates BritRail Senior Pass Senior Flexipass
Greece *212-421-5777*	60 years +	Helenic Railways Pass
Italy *800-248-8687*	60 years +	Carta d'Argento
Luxembourg *212-935-8888*	65 years +	50% off trains and buses
Netherlands Railways *312-819-0300*	60 years +	40% off Senior Card

Scandinavia   55 years +   Scanrail 55+
800-438-7245 or see your travel club or travel agent

- I include Eurailpass and Europass here, even though no senior discount is offered, because both are such good values. Eurailpass offers unlimited First Class train travel throughout most of Western Europe. Special passes for Eastern Europe are now available. Europass is valid for rail travel to France, Germany, Italy, Spain, and Switzerland from 5 to 15 days during a two-month period.
- To qualify for a 50% Austria discount, you must first buy a Railway Senior Citizens ID at any train station. The cost is about $30 and is valid for a calendar year.
- Belgium Golden Railpasses offer six single trips. First Class costs about $80 and Second Class costs about $50.
- French National Railroad sells the Carte Vermeil Quarte Temps card which gives you four reduced-rate trips. The Carte Vermeil Plein Temps cards offers up to a 50% discount within France, and the Plein Temps card for travel from France to other parts of Europe at up to 30% off. Cards cannot be purchased in this country, but are available from French National Railroad in France.
- Scanrail 55+ offers travel in Denmark, Sweden, Norway, and Finland priced as follows:

Any 5 days in 15 days	$193 First Class	$153 Second Class
Any 10 days in 1 month	$301 First Class	$242 Second Class
1 month	$438 First Class	$351 Second Class

These are 1996 prices. As this book goes to print, the 1997 Scanrail pass, Eurailpass, and Flexi pass rates have not been announced. Remember that all passes, unless otherwise noted, are valid for six months. You can buy at the 1996 prices and use your pass in 1997, provided you do so with in six months of the date of purchase.

Senior travel means discount travel. Offers and promotions aimed at the 50 year old + market are coming faster and faster. Your best source of senior discount travel is no different than other discount and promotion offers, viz., travel clubs, senior association newsletters, a good travel agent, news media, and "Just Ask!" The key is knowledge and information. What you don't know, will hurt you!

Chapter 9
Trains
Riding The Rails

To travel by train is to see nature and human beings,
towns and churches and rivers, in fact to see life.
-Agatha Christie

     I do enjoy riding on trains. There is a sense of adventure, of stepping back out of the cyber world we live in, and, for me, a feeling of being connected with where I am going and where I am passing through. I am able to "feel" my travel. I've seen the world from the window of a train in North America, South America, Australia, India, and, of course, all over Europe. What some may see as the disadvantage of train travel, I see as an advantage.

     There are some good savings strategies to lower your train fare. You will find, however, that the cost of train travel in this country is not a bargain on the same scale that air travel is. In many cases, train travel is more expensive than flying. There are some good deals though. As this book goes to press, Amtrak is offering a buy one, get one free offer which equates to a 50 percent discount if two persons are traveling together. (This is a good case in point of my statement in the last chapter on senior discounts suggesting that all senior travelers should not automatically assume that their senior discount is the best deal in town. The current Amtrak offer is giving a 50 percent discount, far more than the senior citizen discount.)

     AMTRAK offers several discount programs, including:
- 15% discount for **senior travelers** ages 62 and over on most services.
- **All Aboard America** fares which divide the country into three regions. Discount fares are based upon peak and off-peak travel.
- **Amtrak Travel Packages** combine train and hotels. Ask Amtrak for their free "Travel Planner."
- **Children's fares** for kids ages 2-15 offer a 50 percent discount when traveling with a full paying adult. Infants less than two years of age travel for free.

- **AirRail Travel Plan** combines Amtrak and United Airlines to offer a rail/fly combination. You train it one way and fly the other. Telephone: 800-321-8684.
- **USA Rail Passes** available to foreign visitors. This pass is similar in concept to a Eurailpass.
- **Ski Amtrak** packages in Utah, Colorado, and Lake Placid, New York. Telephone: 800-841-9800 for Utah and Colorado, and 800-899-2558 for Lake Placid.
- **Seasonal specials and promotions** come and go all year. Ask your travel club or travel agency to keep you posted when a special comes along.

Do you enjoy a nostalgic blast to the past? I love steam engines. Maybe it's the allure of a bygone era; or maybe it just feels good to smell the smoke, feel the steam, and hear the "clackity clack" of the rails. Whatever it is, I love trains, especially steam trains. If you want a real adventure, consider any of these steam train experiences.

- **Cass Scenic Railroad State Park.** Cass, West Virginia. Following an old mountain logging line, the train climbs four miles to Whittaker and then another seven miles to Bald Knob. You have switchbacks and even an 11% grade. Telephone: 304-456-4300
- **Durango & Silverton Narrow-Gauge Railroad.** Durango, Colorado. This is one of the best! Deep river gorges, mountains, peaks, and valleys all make up the 90 mile round-trip to Silverton, Colorado. Plan on a full day. Telephone: 970-247-2733.
- **East Broad Top Railroad.** Rockhill Furnace, Pennsylvania. Operates some of the oldest and most authentic passenger cars in the country, including a business car built in 1880. Telephone: 814-447-3011.
- **Strasburg Rail Road.** Strasburg, Pennsylvania. You will travel four-and-a-half miles through Pennsylvania Dutch and Amish country. Passenger cars have a Victorian-era look and feel; a very popular line. Telephone: 717-687-8628.
- **Valley Railroad Company.** Essex, Connecticut. You ride on the train through the Connecticut River Valley, then switch to a river boat, and then back to the rail cars for your return ride home. Telephone: 203-767-0103.

An excellent book on steam train travel is *31st Annual Steam Passenger Service Directory,* Kalmbach Publishing, P.O. Box 1612, Waukesha, WI 53187.

TRAIN TRAVEL IN EUROPE. Train travel in Europe is fun! Most trains operate efficiently and whisk you from one city to the next at prices far less than air travel. (With the partial de-regulation of Europe airlines and air transportation, we are starting to see a few regional airlines attempt a low cost carrier approach. I hope they succeed.)

Eurailpass. The most famous of all European train passes. This pass gives you virtually unlimited train travel and other travel discounts throughout 17 European countries: Austria, Belgium, Denmark, Finland, France, Germany, Greece, Holland, Hungary, Italy, Luxembourg, Norway, Portugal, Republic of Ireland, Spain, Sweden, and Switzerland. England, Scotland, Wales, and Northern Ireland are not included. Both First Class and Second Class passes are available. First Class allows you to make a reservation and ride in a more comfortable seat and compartment. Your travel period allowance is consecutive days starting on the first day of train travel.

Flexipass offers the convenience of cumulative, not consecutive, travel days.

Saverpass is the same as a Eurailpass, but requires two people traveling together. A discount is given to both passengers. A 15-day First Class Eurailpass costs $522. A 15-day First Class Eurail Saverpass costs $452 each, based on two people traveling together—except from April 1 to September 1, when three people are required to travel together.

Eurail Youthpass is for passengers under 26 years of age as of their first date of travel. If you start traveling on June 1 and turn 26 years old on June 2, you're okay! This pass is for Second Class travel based on consecutive days.

Eurail Youth Flexipass is the same as a Flexipass, except for Second Class travel for passengers less than 26 years of age. Travel days are cumulative.

Europass allows you to travel within France, Germany, Italy, Spain, and Switzerland only. Both First Class and Second Class passes are available.

Europass Youth is the same as Europass, but for passengers less than 26 of age in Second Class.

Europass Drive combines train days and car rental days.

European East Pass allows travel on the national rail networks of Austria, the Czech Republic, Hungary, Poland, and Slovakia.

Individual Country or Regional Passes allow travel in a specific country or area in First Class or Second Class. These passes include the Austrian Railpass, Benelux Tourrail Pass, Bulgarian Flexipass, Czech Flexipass, European East Pass, Finnrail Pass, France Railpass, France Rail 'n Drive Pass, France Rail 'n Fly, France Fly Rail 'n Drive, Germany (Berlin-Nuremberg-Munich itinerary), Hungarian Flexipass, Italy (Rome-Florence-Venice itinerary), Norway Railpass, Portugese Railpass,

RomanianPass, Russian Flexipass, Scanrail Pass, Scanrail 55+, Scanrail 'n Drive, Spain Flexipass, Spain Rail 'n Drive, Swiss Pass, Swiss Flexipass, Swiss Card, Swiss Rail 'n Drive Pass, and the UK France Sampler.

European Rail Passes

Eurailpass	1st Class
15 consecutive days	$ 522
21 consecutive days	$ 678
1 month	$ 838
2 months	$1,148
3 months	$1,468

Eurail Flexipass	1st Class
Any 10 days in 2 months	$ 616
Any 15 days in 2 months	$ 812

Eurail Saverpass	1st Class
15 consecutive days	$ 452
21 consecutive days	$ 578
1 month	$ 712

Eurail Youth Flexipass	2nd Class
Any 10 days in 2 months	$ 438
Any 15 days in 2 months	$ 588

EurailDrive Pass

Any 7 days (4 rail & 3 car) within 2 months + 5 additional rail + additional car days

Car Categories	2 Adults 1st Class	1 Adult 1st Class	Add'l Car Day
Economy	$339	$419	$55
Compact	$379	$479	$75
Intermediate	$389	$509	$85
Add'l rail days (5 max)	$ 55		$55

These are 1996 prices. The 1997 rates have not been released as this book goes to press. Call any of the ticket agents listed below for up-to-date information. Remember, you can use your rail pass, in most cases, up to six months after your date of purchase.

Where can I buy Europe passes and point-to-point tickets?
DER Tours/German Rail   800-421-2929
Rail Europe   800-848-7245
                                           http://www.raileurope.com
                                           800-361-7245 in Canada

Orbis Polish Travel   800-223-6037
Specializes in Eastern Europe

Scantours   800-223-7226
Specializes in Scandinavia

One of the best buys if you're planning to travel in Europe by train. The *Thomas Cook European Timetable*, a complete European train timetable is available from Forsyth Travel Library, 9154 West 57th Street, Shawnee Mission, KS 66201. Telephone: 800-367-7984. Forsyth also sells rail passes.

Eurail Guide, published by Houghton-Mifflin, is an excellent European rail guide.

TRAIN TRAVEL IN GREAT BRITAIN. All BritRail passes offer train travel throughout England, Scotland, and Wales. Ireland may be included at an additional charge. Passes are available in First Class or Standard Class.

BritRail Classic Pass provides First Class or Standard Class travel throughout England, Scotland, and Wales measured consecutively. Commonly referred to as a "BritRail" pass.

BritRail Flexipass measures your travel days cumulatively and is available both in First Class and Standard Class.

BritRail Senior Pass gives seniors ages 60 years and over a 15 percent discount off a First Class BritRail pass.

BritRail Kid's Pass. Buy one adult BritRail or BritRail Senior Pass, and one accompanying child, age 5-15, gets a **FREE** pass of the same type and duration. Additional children purchase the appropriate pass at a 50 discount off the price of a regular adult pass. Children four years and younger travel free. You must ask for the BritRail Kid's Pass when booking.

BritRail Pass + Eurostar. You can book a one-way or round-trip Eurostar journey from London to Paris or Brussels with either a four or eight-day special Flexipass. Train travel is measured cumulatively over a three-month period.

BritRail Pass + Ireland. BritRail pass with Ireland. Round-trip ship passage to Ireland and return is included. If you want to take a car on the crossing, a special discount will be given you for the additional automobile charge.

BritRail Pass + Car. Combination of a BritRail Flexipass and car rental.

BritRail Southeast Pass is a regional pass covering Southeast England. Available in both First Class and Standard Class.

Freedom of Scotland Travelpass offers unlimited rail travel in Scotland on the BritRail network. Available also as a flexipass.

BritRail Passes

Classic Pass

Validity	First Class	Adult Standard	Youth Standard
8 days	$325	$235	$189
15 days	$525	$365	$289
22 days	$665	$465	$369
1 month	$765	$545	$435

Senior Pass

BritRail Senior Flexipass		BritRail Senior Class Pass	
Validity	First Class	Validity	First Class
Any 4 days in 1 month	$245	8 days	$275
Any 8 days in 1 month	$339	15 days	$445
Any 15 days in 1 month	$490	22 days	$565
		1 month	$650

Flexipass

Validity	First Class	Adult Standard	Youth Standard
Any 4 days in 1 month	$289	$199	$160
Any 8 days in 1 month	$399	$280	$225
Any 15 days in 1 month	$615	$425	—
Any 15 days in 2 months	—	—	$340

These are 1996 rates. The 1997 rates have not been released as this book goes to press. Call BritRail for up-to-date information.

Where can I buy BritRail passes and point-to-point tickets?

BritRail Travel International   800-677-8585
212-575-2667
http://www.britrail.co.uk

Which is best, a rail pass or a rental car? That depends on you and where you are planning to go. The train is convenient and you don't have to worry about finding your way from place to place. It also delivers you to the city center of your destination. If you are interested primarily in the larger cities, then train travel is the way to go. If you plan to do more touring in the countryside, you may want to consider a rental car. The number of persons traveling in your party is also a major factor in determining the most economical way to go. For single travelers, train travel will save you money. With two persons, it can be a toss-up. With more than two, rental cars are usually less expensive. Remember, *where* you plan to go is as much a factor as how many persons are in your party.

You should also consider the cost of point-to-point tickets. It may be that a rail pass is not best for you. If your travel will be somewhat limited, call the ticket offices listed with European train travel or BritRail and determine the cost of individual tickets.

As a general rule, you can plan on paying for individual point-to-point tickets as follows:

- 15¢ a mile (12-18¢) for First Class in Bulgaria, the Czech Republic, Poland, Portugal, Slovakia, and Spain; and 10¢ a mile (8-12¢) in Second Class.
- 20¢ a mile (28-22¢) for First Class in Denmark, Finland, Hungary, and Italy; and 13¢ a mile (12-15¢) in Second Class.
- 30¢ a mile (25-35¢) in First Class in Austria, Belgium, France, Greece, Holland, Norway, Romania, and Sweden; and 20¢ (18-22¢) a mile in Second Class.
- 47¢ a mile (37-57¢) in Germany, Great Britain, Ireland, and Switzerland; and 32¢ (30-34¢) a mile in Second Class.

Your train costs will be determined, of course, by where you intend to travel. As an average, figure that individual train tickets will cost you about 29¢ a mile in First Class and 20¢ a mile in Second Class. Now, calculate the number of miles on your itinerary and compare the cost to a rail pass. You can call the ticket offices listed in this section for exact prices.

EUROPE BY BUS. As an alternative to rental car and trains, **Eurobus** offers motor coach transportation to 19 major cities and visitor destinations in Austria, Belgium, the Czech Republic, France, Germany, Hungary, Italy, the Netherlands, and Switzerland. A Eurobus Pass provides unlimited travel over the nine country bus network. At present, Eurobus restricts usage to persons ages 16-38 only. Children less than 16 years and adults ages 39 years or older are not allowed.

Bus travel in Europe is much slower than trains and the seating is rather cramped. The network of available travel areas is smaller and the bus route system is rather limited. Cost is the advantage for the budget minded traveler.

Where can I buy a Eurobus Pass?
Eurotrips   Telephone: 800-517-7778

Eurobus Passes

Validity	Adult	Youth
14 days	$199	$150
1 month	$280	$210
2 months	$350	$275
3 months	$440	$360

These are 1996 rates. The 1997 rates have not been released as this book goes to press. Contact Eurobus for up-to-date information.

Japan Rail Pass. Although little known, the Japan Rail Pass is similar in function to a Eurailpass, except, of course, you are traveling in Japan. Passes are available for both adults and children in Economy Class and First Class. For more information, contact Kintetsu International Express. Telephone: 800-422-3481 or 212-259-9700. E-mail: *Japan@kintetsu.com.* Fax: 212-259-9705.

Chapter 10
How To Travel And Get Paid To Do it!
And I'm Not Kidding!

This is a fun chapter! I am going to tell you one of my best insider secrets. It really works and can be a lot of fun. Thousands of people have done it and keep coming back for more. Ready? Here goes!

Start Your Engines! When was the last time you saw a recreational or speciality vehicle being transported on a truck or train? Probably never. Due to their size, height, weight, construction, and large transportation costs, it is a rarity. These vehicles are usually driven from their manufacturing plant to the tens of thousands of dealerships and customers throughout the United States and Canada.

There are production plants all over the country for recreational and specialty vehicles. California and Indiana, however, are the top two RV producing states. Now, here's the deal. You are accepted as a driver and get yourself to the plant to pick up "your" vehicle. You agree to drive the vehicle and deliver it to a dealer. In most cases, the plant will pay for the gas, hotel costs, and airline ticket home. In some cases, you may even receive payment. Bottom line, you get a "free trip" including return airfare. While some drivers are full time and make a livelihood from this, the majority of drivers are part time and only drive once a year so they can get a "free" vacation. Sometimes the plant will cover the costs, including air, of a traveling companion.

What will you be driving? Anything that does not require a special license. It could be a camper van, RV, ambulance, or just about anything like that. You will know what you are driving and where you are driving to before you go.

A friend of mine did this last spring. He applied and was assigned to pick up an ambulance in Indianapolis and drive it to Salt Lake City. All his expenses, including airfare and meals, were covered, and he was paid to make the delivery.

Here's a great summer deal. Almost all new RVs to Alaska are driven via the Alaska Highway. You pick up the vehicle from the plant somewhere in the lower 48 states (most likely Indiana or California) and drive to Alaska. You are expected to average 350 to 400 miles a day. Your gasoline, hotels, meals, and return air are provided, and you are *paid* to do this!

Can you take your family? Yes, in many cases, but you will have to buy their return airfare and meals. The type of vehicle will also determine if it is appropriate to bring your family along. It can be a great family vacation!

There are only five general requirements.
1. Minimum age of 18. No maximum age.
2. Mature, stable person.
3. Valid driver's license.
4. Relatively good driving record.
5. Reasonably good health.

If you want to know more about this exciting opportunity, buy a copy of *How to Get Paid $30,000 a Year to Travel*, by Craig Chelton. You can order this book from XANADU Enterprises. Telephone: 319-234-0676. The author, Craig Chilton, has been a guest on the *Travel Show*. His interview and explanation of this exciting travel opportunity was one of our best shows.

Cruise Free. Here's another way to travel for free, although you probably won't get paid, but what the heck, you'll cruise free. Ever sit around with friends or family and talk about how much fun it would be to go on a cruise or vacation together?

Well, here's your chance. The Good Book says "The laborer is worthy of his hire." Translation: If you do the work, you enjoy the rewards! Fair enough. Most cruise lines will award one free cruise for every seven cabins sold, or 14 people, assuming two per cabin. When you book 14 cabins, you and your traveling companion cruise for free. You will be responsible, however for port charges. Your airfare may or may not be included depending on the cruise line. You should work with your travel club or travel agency in making these arrangements.

Fly for Free, Tour for Free, and Stay for Free. The same concept exists with airlines, tour companies, and hotels. If you have a group traveling together, always ask about tour conductor passes, known in the travel industry as a "T.C." Ask what the "T.C. ratio" is, and how many free T.C. passes are given with the group of revenue or paying passengers. The answer may be "1 for 15," "1 for 20," "1 for 30," "1 for 40," etc. This translates, "one free ticket for every 15 paying passengers," and so on.

Tour Escorts. Imagine a family guy like me running an escort service! Have you considered serving as a tour escort? It's a lot of work and a lot of fun! You are responsible for a group. This doesn't mean you are necessarily responsible for all the sightseeing commentary, although if you are qualified, you may consider that. Groups organized locally, either by yourself or by a travel agency, may need a guide or escort.

Here are some examples. I have sent more tours to the Holy Land than I can count. I would approach a minister, rabbi, or theology professor and ask him to serve as an escort. This person would share responsibility for signing up tour members.

My "escort" would provide the spiritual or religious commentary on the tour. The trip would be escorted from start to finish by a local guide in Israel, Egypt, and/or Jordan who would provide historical and color commentary. Depending upon our arrangements, my "escort" would receive a free trip and, in some cases, a per person honorarium.

I also contacted university professors and high school teachers to help organize trips all over the world. Their responsibility was to help me plan the trip, sign up tour members, and in many cases, do all or part of the sight-seeing commentary. Some felt comfortable doing it all, others prefer to do part and have "step-on" or "local" guides join the group for a specific day or excursion. In most cases, my "escort" would receive a free trip and honorarium, the latter can easily be a couple thousand dollars or more. Not a bad summer job!

You may wish to serve only as an escort or tour manager and not be responsible for any tour sales. In this case, you will most likely receive your trip and basic expenses free, but probably not be paid. How would you find an escort job? Assuming you are interested in doing this on an *ad hoc* basis and not as a full-time job, here's what to do:

- Do you know a travel agent, preferably an office manager? Ask him/her about organizing and/or escorting a tour group.
- Put together a brief resumé with your personal and professional back ground. Highlight your previous travels, where you've been, language skills, references, and any prior experience. If you can, take this in person to a travel agency manager and introduce yourself. Travel agents who organize tours are always looking for good escorts.
- If you are willing to help organize and sell a tour, you're in! Every travel company is looking to acquire new business. If you have a group of people or the potential of a group, you are the agency's meal ticket!

Remember, *you* are doing the work and *you* deserve to be taken care of.

Get Yourself Bumped and Fly For FREE. Airlines, cruise lines, hotels, and car rentals companies routinely take more reservations than they have available space. In other words, if everyone shows up, they're in deep kimchi! Based upon historical data and yield management reports, airline suppliers have a very accurate prediction of what their actual load factor will be. In a few instances, more people show up who have confirmed reservations than there are available seats. The national average of denied boardings per 10,000 passengers due to overbooked flights is 1.18.[33]

Airline Denied Boarding ("Bumped") Due To Overbooked Flights per 10,000 Passengers

Top 3: Fewest Bumped Passengers[34]

Continental	0.23
American	0.43
Northwest	0.55
National Average	1.18

Bottom 3: Most Bumped Passengers[35]

Southwest	2.74
Alaska	2.56
America West	1.96
National Average	1.18

When an airline has overbooked a flight, no passengers will be denied boarding until "volunteers" have been sought who will give up their seat in exchange for compensation at the airline's discretion. Typically, the compensation is a round-trip ticket on that carrier within the 48 states. (Remember, involuntary denied boarding compensation is a whole different ball game! You can accept the airline compensation, or ask for compensation as specified by the government. Ask for a copy of the airline's Denied Boarding Compensation statement.)

Some years ago a friend, who was the Sports Editor for one of the local newspapers, and I were flying to Honolulu. He was going to cover a couple of basketball games in Hawaii. (Tough job, huh?) I was tagging along just for fun. We flew from Salt Lake City to San Francisco and boarded our United Airlines flight to Honolulu. Just a few minutes before our scheduled departure, the gate agent announced over the p.a. that the flight was overbooked and asked if anyone was interested in giving up their seat in exchange for a free round-trip ticket anywhere United flew in the contiguous 48 states; the volunteers would be accommodated on the next flight. We looked at each other, nodded, and said, "I'm in!" As we approached the agent I said to my friend, "Let me handle this one."

The first question I always ask in this situation is, "When is the next flight you can put us on?"

"In about three hours," she replied.

Second question I always ask, "Can you guarantee me a seat or will I be stand-by?" Your willingness to volunteer may change if you have to travel stand-by, not knowing when you may get to your final destination, or if you will even get there that day.

"Yes, I can guarantee you a seat on our next flight," she said.

Usually if the wait is more than a couple of hours, the airline will throw in a meal voucher and a telephone call so you can notify friends, family, or business associates that you are delayed.

Just as she started to lead us off the plane and back into the terminal, I said, "We'll be happy to volunteer if you will upgrade us to First Class on the next flight." If there are many volunteers, your bargaining power is limited. If there are fewer volunteers than needed, you may be able to negotiate with them. (What agent wants to face angry passengers nervously waiting in the terminal hoping to get on their flight for which they have confirmed reservations?) If you decide to negotiate a better deal, be reasonable and don't be a jerk about it.

The rest of the story. We each picked up a free round-trip domestic ticket anywhere United flew within the 48 states and a First Class ticket for the next flight. A good deal in my book!

Cathy and I were returning from a three-day weekend trip to our favorite city, San Francisco. As we waited to board our 3:00 p.m. Delta flight home, the gate agent asked if anyone was interested in giving up their seat in exchange for, you got it.....a free round trip ticket anywhere they fly in the 48. The next flight was at 4:30 p.m. and volunteers we guaranteed a seat. Not a bad deal!

If you are interested in volunteering, ask the gate agent if the flight is heavily booked and, if so, will they possibly be needing "volunteers." If the agent anticipates a possible need for friendly volunteers, he/she will take your name and ask you to remain in the departure area while the flight boards. If you are needed, you will be called. If not, you will be asked to board the plane. (Darn it, now all the overhead space is gone!) Caution: if you have not been called and the scheduled departure time is near, ask the agent what your status is as a volunteer. In the rush to get a flight out, there have been a few passengers, hoping to volunteer, not called because they were not needed, and the agent forgot to tell them to board, and now they have missed their original flight. Bummer!

Get Yourself Walked and Stay for Free. Hotels face the same dilemma as airlines. How many reservations will really show up?

I arrived at the Atlanta Marriott Airport Hotel late one night. My room was "guaranteed for late arrival" with my credit card. This means my room will be held; it is guaranteed. Upon check-in, I was told the hotel was full and could not accommodate me.

"My reservation is guaranteed for late arrival," I told the front desk clerk.

"I'm sorry Mr. Gelwix. Although your room is guaranteed, we are sold out. We have made reservations for you at a nearby hotel and will provide transportation to the hotel and cover the cost of your room."

It's now about one o'clock in the morning and what I really wanted was a bed. I accepted the offer (what could I do, sleep in the lobby?), went to the other hotel, and got a free room. (Dang, why didn't I ask for breakfast, too? Momentarily lapse due to fatigue I guess.)

Here's a question I wanted to ask J. Willard, "What does 'guarantee' mean?" I did ask the agent this question, "Your hotel is full tonight. Every room is taken and there is no room in the inn, right?"

"That's correct. Sorry." she answered.

"Okay, my room was guaranteed with my credit card. Your hotel is full. Suppose I didn't show up tonight, even though you had sold my room, would I have been charged for the room because I was a 'no-show?'"

She paused, thought about it, smiled, and said nothing. I think I knew the answer.

Just remember, as frustrating and aggravating as getting "walked" can be, keep your cool. We've all seen some idiot shouting and cursing at an airline, hotel, or car rental agent. The poor agent didn't overbook the flight or hotel. Hopefully, he/she is trying to help you.

There is a time to be firm, but firm does not allow you to be arrogant or rude. Case in point, two months ago I was returning from Samoa. My wife, daughter, and I were booked on Polynesian Airlines, which shares a flight to Honolulu with Air New Zealand. "Poly" (as Polynesian Airlines is called) requires that all passengers re-confirm their flights at least 72 hours prior to departure or risk losing their reservation. I re-confirmed all three of us. For unknown reasons, upon check-in at Faleolo Airport for our flight to Honolulu, Poly showed my wife and I re-confirmed, but no dice for my daughter Emily. (Now how does this happen?) My 16 year-old daughter was told she would have to wait as a "stand-by," but Mom and Dad could go ahead and board. Right!

Problem #1, the flight was heavily overbooked and the chances of getting on were somewhere between negligible and nil. Problem #2, there is only one flight a week. If Emily didn't make it, we would all be staying.

Problem #3, no way could I leave without my daughter.

What to do? No time to be a wall flower here. No excuse to be rude either. The Poly agent was doing her job. Whatever happened to Emily's re-confirmation, which was done at the same time as mine, was not this agent's fault. I asked to speak to the supervisor. I explained our dilemma. He explained there was little he could do. I didn't let it go at that, but still pressed my case. Eventually I was invited to Poly's private office behind the counter. I telephoned Poly in Los Angeles. After some more nervous moments, I was given three boarding passes for the flight. Emily was moved to the head of the class and somehow by-passed the waiting list! I attribute this to a combination of my polite persistence and the good graces of the Poly supervisor. I know that if I had started shouting and waving my arms around, Emily never would have made that flight. I also know if I had just accepted what I was told, let it go at that, and sat around hoping for the waiting list to clear, she would not have made the flight either.

I have an intense love affair with the South Pacific. I have traveled throughout Polynesia. I sailed to distant and remote islands where people cling to traditional lifestyles and life has remained almost unchanged. Robert Louis Stevenson was also drawn to the South Seas and eventually settled in Samoa. Stevenson captured the essence of my feelings when he wrote in 1888:

Few men who come to the islands leave them; they grow grey where they alighted; the palm shades and the trade-wind fans them till they die, perhaps cherishing to the last the fancy of a visit home, which is rarely made, more rarely enjoyed, and yet more rarely repeated. No part of the world exerts the same attractive power upon the visitor, and the task before me is to communicate to fireside travelers some sense of its seduction....

The first experience can never be repeated. The first love, the first sunrise, the first South Sea island, are memories apart and touched a virginity of sense.[36]

Get Bumped and Cruise for Free. Cruise lines face the same problem. Too many reservations that make final payment. It's tougher for cruise lines to accommodate "oversells" than for airlines or hotels. Cruise companies can't say, "We'll put you on the another sailing in a few hours."

Typical offers that are made to cruise passengers who voluntarily give up their cabin on an oversold sailing are alternate cruise dates with a partial refund, a longer cruise at no extra charge, a full refund, and/or a credit or discount on a future cruise. In some cases, when the sailing date is close and there are still confirmed passengers without cabins, you may receive an offer for a full refund and a free cruise at a future date. Fortunately, offers to "get bumped" on a cruise are usually made several days, sometimes even weeks, in advance, before you leave home. There are a few isolated cases where passengers have been bumped at the pier, but this is rare.

It is unlikely that you will talk directly to the cruise line as your reservation was probably booked with a travel club or travel agency. Your booking agent will relay the offers to you. If your time is flexible, take the offer.

A couple of years ago we booked ourselves and a group of friends on a *Crystal Harmony* sailing from New York City to Bermuda, St. Thomas, and San Juan, Puerto Rico. Several weeks prior to our departure, Crystal advised us that the cruise was oversold and asked if we would be interested in "trading" our one week cruise for a 10-day cruise that included passage through the Panama Canal. Volunteers would also be upgraded to deluxe cabins or suites. Both the longer cruise and upgrade were be provided at no additional cost. It was a good offer and several in our group decided to go for it.

Chapter 11
Courier Travel
Get Ready, Get Set, Go!...Today

I am fortunate to be asked to speak to many conventions, conferences, meetings, and groups all over the country and overseas. I genuinely enjoy meeting people and particularly enjoy the Q&A sessions and individual "chit-chat" with attendees. There are several questions that seem to be asked at every meeting. One of these is about courier travel.

An air courier, sometimes called a casual courier, is a person who will take whatever needs to be transported and "carry" the commodity on an international flight. A courier doesn't actually carry or handle anything other than a piece of paper called a "manifest," which identifies whatever has been checked in as luggage by the courier company. The most common shipments are documents, but may include just about anything....anything legal, that is! Usually the air courier will only be allowed to take carry-on luggage as the check-in luggage allowance is needed for the shipment.

To better explain air courier travel, I have listed the most frequently asked questions and answers:

Now just what do I do as an air courier? In exchange for a discounted international airline ticket, your check-in luggage allowance will be used by the shipping company. You travel when the contracting company needs you and on the flights they pick.

You meet the courier company representative at the airport at a predetermined time and receive an "On Board Courier Pouch," or manifest for "your" luggage and its contents. You are not paid as a courier. The courier company pays part of your ticket in exchange for your "services."

Why do companies use couriers? Luggage sent overseas as air freight may often sit in the Arrival Customs office for days or weeks. Luggage taken by passengers goes through Arrival Customs with the passenger — you. In many cases, it is less expensive for a company to subsidize a passenger's ticket than to pay air freight costs. Couriers typically transport time sensitive materials such as documents, supplies, equipment, and so on. Anything that needs to get to its destination quickly with little or no chance of a foul-up. Whatever is being sent along with you is checked in by the courier company as luggage using your ticket. In one sense, you are the tag-along!

Can anyone become an air courier? Almost anyone. Most people will qualify. There is an image of couriers as young, single, carefree wanderers with backpacks. Actually, most couriers are adults who just love to travel at a discount.

Couriers must be at least 18 years old (a few companies require their couriers to be 21 years), possess a valid passport, and be levelheaded. You should wear neat clothing — no hippy or grungy look. Some companies ask that you do not drink alcohol while on board as you are representing them.

Am I an employee of the courier company? No. You are receiving compensation in the form of a subsidized airline ticket in exchange for your courier services. You are known as a "casual courier" or "freelance courier." Your services are those of an independent contractor.

So tell me the process. First, contact one of the companies looking for couriers. You can join one of the organizations or associations that publish listings of courier flights, contact a courier broker, or contact a courier company direct.

Here's the lingo you need to know:

Courier	Someone ("you") who agrees to deliver something. In this context, you accompany the courier company's luggage on your ticket. Your delivery is accompanying the shipment that has been checked-in as luggage.
Courier Broker	A third party that acts as a booking agent for courier companies.
Courier Company	A delivery company that contracts with couriers ("you").

There are several associations (see the end of this chapter) that contact courier companies to find out what courier needs are coming up. The association then notifies its members and the members ("you") contact the courier company in hopes of securing a seat. Some consider it convenient to join an association, but it is not necessary. Associations do not book your courier flights, but do advise you of what courier flights are available. If you join an association, ask how often courier flight notices are updated and sent to members. You pay an annual membership fee.

A courier broker is a booking agent for one or more courier companies. You contact them and find out what is available. There is often a fee charged by the courier broker for his services. Unlike an association which only advises you of what is available, a broker can usually confirm your flight. Many brokers represent more than one company and can advise you of what flights are available.

You may also contact the courier company direct. Some will book you on the spot, some may ask you to leave your name and number and they will call you when a need arises, and some will ask that you deal with a broker that represents them. Courier companies are in the shipping and delivery business, not the travel business.

After you have been accepted, the courier company or broker will advise you of your flight schedule and where and when to meet their representative. The meeting is usually at the departure airport two to three hours prior to flight time. You receive your tickets at that time.

You will be met at your destination airport and deliver whatever you are accompanying at the other end. The delivery will always take place at the arrival airport. In most cases, your delivery consists of handing over the manifest and luggage claim checks to the courier company's agent.

You receive a round-trip ticket and are told when you will return. Often, but not always, you will accompany a courier shipment home.

What is the cost? Usually $200-$450; sometimes more, sometimes less. You are paying part of your ticket cost and the courier company is paying part of it. Most courier companies try to get half of the ticket price covered by the courier. During the busy summer months, the rates will be higher than in winter. Free flights are sometimes available, but it is rare. All expenses during your overseas stay are your responsibility.

Actually, the cost of the ticket is sometimes negotiable. When a courier need is posted, a price is listed. If the need is not filled, the price will start to drop as the departure date gets closer. Within 24 and 48 hours of departure, everything is negotiable. Last-minute couriers can find fares as low at $99 round-trip to Europe or Asia. These last minute courier rates are the exception, rather than the rule.

How many courier flights are available each year? About 40,000. Not only are flights available from the United States and Canada to overseas destination, but there are many courier flights originating in foreign countries to other foreign destinations.

How far in advance can I book? The need for couriers is posted anywhere from 24 hours to three months prior to departure. Flights to popular destinations usually require two to three months notice on your part during peak travel months. Many flights can be booked within a few weeks of departure. There are "last minute" courier offers also, like "Can you leave tomorrow?"

How do I know I'm not escorting something illegal? Deal with established, reputable firms. Actually, you never even touch, lift, or handle "your" luggage. It is delivered to you at the airport check-in counter and a receiving agent takes it at the other end. You show the manifest to the customs officer at your destination.

Do I get to choose where I will be going as a courier? Yes. You review the courier postings and apply only for those going to your preferred destinations.

What airlines are used? All the major carriers. You should join the frequent flyer program of whatever airline you fly, or check the airline frequent flyer partners in Appendix 1. For example, suppose you fly Singapore Airlines from San Francisco to Hong Kong (round-trip courier fare is about $350 and a "last minute" courier fare is about $100....yes, you read that right!) The published round-trip tariffs are $880 to $1,260, depending on the season of travel. You may wish to join Singapore's Passages Frequent Flyer Programme, or figuring that you probably won't have the pleasure of flying Singapore Airlines too much, take your frequent flyer miles with Delta Air Lines. Delta and Singapore have a reciprocal mileage agreement. The actual round-trip flight mileage San Francisco/Hong Kong is 13,802. That is more than halfway to a free Delta domestic ticket, and you didn't even fly Delta!

What cities do courier flights depart from? The major gateway cities, include Chicago, Houston, Los Angeles, Miami, New York City, San Francisco, and San Juan, P.R. Sometimes you will also find some flights originating in Dallas, Washington, D.C., and other cities. Your return flight will be back to the city from which you departed, unless you make open jaw arrangements.

Courier flights originating in foreign countries to other non-U.S. international destinations include Argentina, Australia, Canada, Ecuador, England, France, Germany, Guatemala, Hong Kong, Japan, Mexico, Singapore, and Thailand.

Where do couriers fly to? Just about everywhere in the world. Flights include most major cities in Europe, Asia, South America, Australia, New Zealand, Africa, Mexico, and the Middle East.

How long will I stay? This is usually determined by the needs of the courier company, as you may be acting as a courier on your return flight also. The average is two to three weeks. Some stays are less than a week, some can be up to 90 days, and some are even longer! The longer stays are the result of a request to the courier company for an extended stay. You will know your travel dates and length of stay when you sign up and are accepted as a courier.

After I am accepted, is it my responsibility to get myself to the departure city? Yes. It is much easier to serve as a courier if you live in a gateway city. If you do not live in a gateway city, it is your responsibility to get yourself there. Don't cut the connection time close. Courier companies usually require you to be at the airport two or three hours prior to departure. If you are flying into your gateway departure city, allow yourself six to eight hours in case your flight is delayed, or worse, canceled. If you miss your courier flight, you won't get a second chance!

If you do not live in a gateway departure city, you should compare the cost of a consolidator ticket from your home city to your international destination to the combined cost of your courier ticket and your connecting ticket from your hometown to your overseas departure city. In some cases, the cost of a consolidator ticket from a non-courier gateway city will be less.

Do I travel alone? That's up to you. The courier company's need may be just for one person on a particular flight. Your traveling companion(s) can buy a ticket on your flight or just meet you at the other end. Sometimes you will be advised of your airline and flight number weeks in advance; other times you will know only a few days before you leave.

If you are traveling with a companion, you should both apply for the same flight. Sometimes more than one courier is needed. Or, apply for the same day of travel to the same destination, but with different companies. You can also travel one day and your companion fly as a courier the day before or the day after.

What are the advantages of flying as a courier? Only one. In most cases, you will save some money on your ticket cost. You can also avoid some advance purchase restrictions inasmuch as the courier company will arrange your ticket.

What are the disadvantages? You give up your check-in luggage, often you are unable to change your itinerary, and sometimes a loss of frequent flyer miles. There is a possibility that your courier travel dates and itinerary may be changed or canceled by the contracting company sometime prior to your departure, although this is unlikely.

You must make a judgement on the company you will be acting as a courier for. There are a few horror stories about stranded passengers, scam companies that advertise cheap couriers flights and then disappear with the money, and contraband in the luggage. These occurrences are, however, isolated and uncommon.

Most contracting companies are reputable businesses. If you are responsible and trustworthy, you may be put on a "preferred courier list." Their business is dependent upon delivering the goods and they are always looking for good people.

It is sometimes easier to find a courier flight by visiting the company offices in person. If you do not live in one of the gateway cities, you can contact them by telephone, fax, or mail. As mentioned earlier, courier travel is best suited for those living in or near a gateway city.

Is courier travel for everyone? Probably not. If you are flexible and not pressed for time, you can save some money and have some fun in the process. If you think you might want to give courier travel a try, pick up a copy of Mark Field's *The Complete Air Travel Handbook*, published by Perpetual Press. This excellent book provides an extensive list of courier companies and brokers both in the United States, Canada, and overseas, along with information on budget accommodations when you arrive at your destination, or join the Air Courier Association.

Reference Books:

The Air Courier's Handbook. Big City Books, P.O. Box 19667, Sacramento, CA 95819.

The Courier Air Travel Handbook. Mark Field. Perpetual Press. P.O. Box 45628, Seattle, WA 98145-0628. Telephone: 800-937-8000.

Directory of Freelance On Board Couriers. The Inside Track Travel Group, British Columbia. Telephone: 604-684-6715.

The Insiders Guide To Air Courier Bargains. Inwood Training Publications, P.O. Box 438, New York City, NY 10034.

Newsletters:

Travel Unlimited. $25 annual fees. 12 issues. Steve Lantos, P.O. Box 1058, Allston, MA 02134-1058.

Associations:

Air Courier Association. 191 University Blvd., Suite 300, Denver, CO 80206. Telephone: 303-279-3600. Fax: 303-278-1293. Membership fee of $30 plus annual dues of $28. (First year membership is $58 and then the annual dues thereafter.)

International Association of Air Travel Couriers. P.O. Box 1349, Lake Worth, FL 33460. Telephone: 561-582-8320. Fax: 561-582-1581. E-mail: *iaatc@courier.org*   Annual fee of $35.

World Courier Association. Telephone: 716-527-0648.

Courier Companies:

Chicago	Jupiter	708-298-3850	Asia, Europe
Houston	Now Voyager	212-431-1616	Europe
Los Angeles	Halbert Express	718-656-8189	Australia
	I.B.C.[37]	310-607-0125	Asia
	Jupiter Air	310-670-5123	Australia
	Midnight Express	310-672-1100	Europe

Miami	Halbert Express	305-593-0260	South America
	I.B.C.	305-591-8080	South America
	Linehaul Services	305-477-0651	Europe, South America
	Trans-Air System	305-592-1771	South America
New York	Air Facility	718-712-1769	Europe, South America
	Courier Network	212-691-9860	Israel
	East West Express	718-656-6242	Asia, Australia
	Halbert Express	718-656-8189	Asia, Europe
	Jupiter Air	718-656-6050	Asia, Europe
	Now Voyager	212-431-1616	Africa, Asia, Europe, Mexico, South America
	World Courier	516-354-2600	Europe, Mexico
San Francisco	Jupiter Air	415-872-0845	Asia, Europe
	UTL Travel	415-583-5074	Asia

Air Courier Brokers:

Discount Travel	212-362-3636
Courier Travel	516-763-6898
Now Voyager	212-431-1616
Way To Go	213-466-1126

Chapter 12
Just A Little Fun Stuff!
Travel Trivia And Other Junk.

Lost In Translation!

Sometimes translating from one language to another doesn't convey the correct meaning. Here are some messages mistranslated into English from around the world.

Copenhagen airline ticket office: *We take your bags and send them in all directions.*

Yugoslavian hotel: *The flattening of underwear with pleasure is the job of the chambermaid.*

Swiss restaurant: *Our wines will leave you nothing to hope for.*

Zurich hotel: *Because of the impropriety of entertaining guests of the opposite sex in the bedroom, it is suggested that the lobby be used for this purpose.*

Hotel elevator in Paris: *Please leave your values at the front desk.*

Announcement in Soviet Weekly: *There will be a Moscow Exhibition of Arts by 1,500 Soviet Republic painters and sculptures. These were executed over the past two years.*

Tokyo hotel: *It is forbidden to steal hotel towels, please. If you are not a person to do such a thing, it is easier not to read this. Please bathe inside the tub.*

Bucharest, Romania, hotel lobby: *The lift* [elevator] *is being fixed for the next day. During that time we regret that you will be unbearable.*

Moscow hotel door: *If this is your first visit to Russia, you are welcome to it.*

Hotel in Japan: *You are invited to take advantage of the chambermaid.*

Dry cleaners in Thailand: *Drop your trousers here for best results.*

Russian hotel: *You are welcome to visit the cemetary where famous Russian and Soviet composers, artists, and writers are buried daily except Thursday.*

Budapest zoo: *Please do not feed the animals. If you have any suitable food, give it to the guard on duty.*

Car rental brochure in Tokyo: *When passengers of foot heave in sight, tootle the horn. Trumpet him melodiously at first, but if he still obstacles your passage, then tootle him with vigor.*

Athens hotel: *Visitors are expected to complain at the office between the hours of 9 and 11 a.m. daily.*

Hong Kong dentist's ad: *Teeth extracted by the latest Methodists.*

****

Whose Got The Best Wine Cellar In The Sky?

Business Traveler International magazine asked 25 professional wine judges to sample and rate 140 wines voluntarily submitted by 29 airlines from their Business Class wine lists. Here are the winners:[38] What do you think?

1. Delta Air Lines
2. Austrian Airlines
3. Air New Zealand
4. KLM Royal Dutch Airlines (tie)
   Virgin Atlantic (tie)
6. SAS
7. Air India
8. American Airlines
9. TWA
10. Sabena Belgian Airlines

****

Social Manners On An Airplane

Have any of these situations ever happened to you? A recent survey of business travelers on their inflight behavior responded to the following statements.[39]

Changed seats on a flight to avoid the person you were sitting next to:
      Men   38%   Women 40%

Asked at check-in to be seated away from other passengers if possible:
      Men   22%   Women 22%

Met someone on a flight with whom you formed a personal relationship:
      Men   20%   Women 18%

Asked at check-in to be seated next to someone you wanted to meet:
      Men   19%   Women 14%

Complained to the crew about your neighbor's behavior:
      Men   9%   Women 11%

Suffered sexual harassment on a flight:
      Men   0%   Women 9%

****

More Lost In Translation!

If I wasn't in the travel business, I think I would be a food critic. My favorite meal? Dim sum Chinese. Seafood, Indian, and Thai are right behind. I particularly enjoy sampling the local cuisine wherever my travels take me. Here are some menu items from around the world that seemed to suffer a bit when translated into English.

Cairo:	*Muscles of Marines and lobster thermos*
Hong Kong:	*Indonesian Nazi Goreng*
Japan:	*Buttered saucepans and fried hormones*
Poland:	*Beef rashers beaten up in the country peoples' fashion*
Europe:	*Sweat from the trolley*
China:	*Cold shredded children and sea blubber in spicy sauce*
Bali:	*Toes with butter and jam*
Japan:	*Fried fisherman*
Europe:	*Dreaded veal cutlet with potatoes and cream*
Japan:	*Teppan Yaki -- before your cooked right eyes*

Driving Mom And Dad Crazy!
What do kids do that drive their parents nuts?

Sea World/Busch Gardens asked children ages 8 to 12 what kids do on family vacations that drive their parents crazy.[40] Are your kids "normal?"

Fighting with siblings..52%
Asking, "Are we there yet?"...............................30%
Singing songs...4%
Telling silly jokes..4%
Always asking for a bathroom stop 3%
Getting carsick...3%

Only the top 6 responses were reported.

****

The *Perfect* Family Vacation

Now it's the parents turn. Amtrak and the Travel Industry Association conducted a survey of adults on what makes for a perfect family vacation.[41] Are you "normal?"

What We Like

To see and learn something new..........................43%
Time with and without children...........................22%
To arrive still speaking..18%
Meeting interesting people...................................10%
Someone else to deal with traffic..........................7%

What We Don't Like

Road construction and traffic...............................32%
Bored children...24%
Getting lost..23%
Looking for a place to eat or sleep......................14%
Too much togetherness...7%

Kids Ultimate Vacations

Children ages 8 to 12 were asked what they would like as the best, coolest, neatest, radist, most awesome, ultimate vacation. Here are their responses:[42]

Coast-to-coast theme park tour..............................25%
Trip under the ocean...21%
African safari...18%
Trip into space...17%
Mountain climbing in Alaska................................14%

****

Most Popular Theme Parks In America[43]

Rank	Park	Attendance in Millions	% Change 1994/1995
1.	Disneyland *Anaheim, CA*	14.10	38%
2.	Magic Kingdom *Orlando, FL*	12.90	15%
3.	Epcot *Orlando, FL*	10.70	10%
4.	Disney-MGM Studios *Orlando, FL*	9.50	19%
5.	Universal Studios Florida *Orlundo, FL*	8.00	4%
6.	Sea World *Orlando, FL*	4.95	7.5%
7.	Universal Studios *Hollywood, CA*	4.70	2%
8.	Six Flags Great Adventure *Jackson, NJ*	4.00	25%
9.	Busch Gardens *Tampa, FL*	3.80	3%
10.	Sea World *San Diego, CA*	3.75	up slightly

Are You An Average Joe?

The average American has visited 16 states, according to the Travel Industry Association. Ninety-nine percent have left their home state at least once, while only two percent have visited all 50 states.

Who travels the most? The study found residents of the mountain states, senior citizens, and adults without children to be the most active travelers.[44]

****

You're Not Serious, Are You?

Here are some interesting questions asked at tourist offices:

Florida:	*Which beach is closet to the ocean?*
New Orleans:	*When is your next jazz funeral?*
Idaho:	*If we eat in a restaurant in Idaho and don't order a potato, will we be asked to leave?*
Hawaii:	*What language do you speak in Hawaii?*
Arizona:	*Have we made peace with the Indians yet?*
Colorado:	*What is the best time of year to watch deer turn into elk?*
Alaska:	*Do you have a map of the Iditarod Trail? I would like to go for a walk this afternoon.*

At my travel agency, we were asked by a woman who objected to buying a ticket for her two year-old child, "Can I put him in the overhead compartment or under my seat?" (Yes, she was serious!)

Most families want to sit together on the plane. One family of six was traveling to Hawaii and specifically asked our agent not to sit any member of the family together. The agent jokingly asked why vacation together if you don't like each other? "Oh, we love each other very much," the father replied. "But in case we're in a crash, if we're seated all over the plane, at least one of us may survive."

Okay!

I remember the woman who asked to have a window seat on her upcoming flight because, as she explained, "I get air sick and I want to sit by a window so I can get some fresh air."

Oh I get it, roll the window down! Why didn't I think of that?

"What's the best way to fly to Germany," a caller on the *Travel Show* asked. "On an airplane," I replied.

****

Travel Insurance Claims

Travel insurance companies have heard it all. Here are some claims that were submitted, deemed valid, and paid on:[45]

An air conditioner vent fell out of the wall on a cruise ship, hitting a man on the heard while he was sitting on the toilet.

A cape buffalo ran over a man while he was on a safari.

A herd of donkeys attacked a woman while she was vacationing in Greece.

A cable carrying luggage to a cruise ship broke, sending all of the luggage into the harbor.

A large rat allegedly ran off with a man's dentures and hearing aid that were lying on the night stand in his hotel room. (Nice hotel!)

A man, who was saving a person from drowning, had his wallet and watch stolen from the beach.

****

What Are The Busiest Air Routes?

We all want to get away from it all and follow a road less traveled, but you won't find it here. Listed below are the busiest air routes in the country, called city pairs, according to the Air Transport Association. City pairs are rank ordered with #1, New York/Los Angeles and vice versa, being the busiest as measured by number of passengers. Cover the answers and guess the top five.

1.	New York City	Los Angeles
2.	New York City	Chicago
3.	Honolulu	Kahului, Maui
4.	New York City	Miami
5.	New York City	Boston
6.	Dallas/Fort Worth	Houston
7.	New York City	San Francisco
8.	New York City	Washington, D.C.
9.	New York City	Orlando

10.	Los Angeles	Las Vegas
11.	Los Angeles	San Francisco
12.	New York City	Atlanta
13.	Honolulu	Lihue, Kauai
14.	New York City	Fort Lauderdale
15.	Los Angeles	Oakland
16.	New York City	San Juan, P.R.
17.	Chicago	Detroit
18.	New York City	West Palm Beach
19.	Los Angeles	Honolulu
20.	Los Angeles	Phoenix

****

High-Tech Carry-ons And Other Business Toys

What are the favorite high-tech carry-on items of business travelers?[46] Does it vary from country to country? Take a look.

Country	Personal Computer	Cellular Phone	Pager
United Kingdom	67%	53%	6%
United States	62%	28%	24%
Germany	57%	50%	–
Japan	42%	15%	5%

****

Travel Agents Gender Mix[47]
National Average
Women agents..............................64%
Men agents..................................36%

Small Travel Agencies
$1 million or less annual sales
Women agents............................. 71%
Men agents................................. 29%

Large Travel Agencies
$5 million or more annual sales

Women agents.............................51%
Men agents.................................49%

****

International Relations

- Bowing in Japan is a sign of respect. Who bows first? How low do you go? That is, how low do you bow? The answer to both questions is rank. In Japanese society, especially business, it is critically important to know the rank of the person you are dealing with. Therefore, the higher the rank of the person you meet, the lower you bow. So, who bows first and lowest? The person of lower rank.

- In America, if you want to signal that everything is okay, you give a thumbs-up gesture. Some believe the origin of this gesture goes back to ancient Rome. The emperor would signal whether a gladiator should live or die by a "thumbs up" or "thumbs down." Others discount this story. Whatever the origin, the "thumbs up" for Americans means everything is fine. In Australia, this gesture means "up yours." In Nigeria, it is viewed as a rude gesture.

- In America, if you want to signal your agreement, you nod your head up and down. To say no, you shake it back and forth. In Bulgaria, and parts of Greece, Yugoslavia, Turkey, and Iran, the reverse is true. Nodding the head up and down means "no." Shaking the head back and forth means "yes."

- Eating with your left hand in India is considered uncoth.

****

True Love?

Club Med recently conducted a survey of couples regarding "romance and romantic moments" at their properties in the Bahamas, the Caribbean, and Mexico.[48] Here are some of the results:

- 63% of couples who had been married five years or more and only 18% of unmarried couples identified "spending time together" as the most enjoyable aspect of their vacation.
- Couples who had been married for more than five years held hands and walked on the beach 10 times more often than newlyweds.
- Couples who did *not* diet while on vacation had three times more romantic moments during their vacation than couples who were dieting.
- Those couples who were dieting were three times more likely to argue than couples not dieting. (Could there be a lesson here?)
- Couples who had chocolate for dessert said they went to bed, on average, at 12:53 a.m., while those who preferred fruit for desert went to bed, on average, at 10:30 p.m.
- Couples who played tennis against each other were three times more likely to have a romantic moment than those couples who played on the same team.

****

Lost In Space

Doesn't it drive you crazy to keep waiting for your luggage to come down the shoot and it never seems to appear? The national average for mishandled luggage is 5.18 pieces per 1,000 passengers. Here is how airlines stack up,[49] with #1 being the best record with the least number of missing bags.

Rank:	Airline:	Reports per 1,000 Passengers:
1.	Southwest[50]	4.26
2.	Continental	4.69
3.	America West	4.82
4.	USAir	4.90
5.	American	5.08
	National Average	5.18
6.	United	5.23
7.	Delta	5.28
8.	Alaska	5.75
9.	Northwest	6.33
10.	TWA	6.37

Best Airport On-Time Performace

A flight is considered "on-time" if it operates within 15 minutes of its schedule. Mechanical delays, once included in on-time performance reports, are now excluded for fear that some airlines may "shave" mechanical work to boast on-time ratings. The on-time performance of individual flights is listed in CRS displays. Ask your travel agent or travel club to advise you on your flight's on-time performance.

Listed below are the on-time airport's arrival and departure ratings.[51] You are more likely to be delayed in some airports than others.

Arrivals		Departures	
__Airport:__	__% On-Time__	__Airport:__	__% On-Time:__
1. Cincinnati	82.3	1. Washington National	86.5
2. Charlotte	81.7	2. Orlando	86.2
3. Minneapolis	81.7	3. Houston Intercon.	85.7
4. Detroit	81.5	4. Tampa	85.2
5. Denver	81.2	5. New York LaGuardia	84.7
6. Houston Intercon.	81.2	6. Seattle	83.7
7. Pittsburgh	81.0	7. Philadelphia	83.7
8. Dallas/Ft. Worth	80.7	8. San Diego	83.6
9. New York LaGuardia	80.6	9. Minneapolis	83.3
10. Washington National	79.8	10. Cincinnati	83.1
11. Philadelphia	79.8	11. Miami	83.1
12. Las Vegas	79.2	12. Denver	82.0
13. Phoenix	79.1	13. Boston	82.0
14. Chicago O'Hare	79.0	14. Newark	81.6
15. Salt Lake City	78.1	15. Pittsburgh	81.4
16. San Diego	77.8	16. New York Kennedy	81.2
17. Orlando	77.3	17. Phoenix	81.1
18. Miami	76.1	18. Las Vegas	81.1
19. St. Louis	75.9	19. Charlotte	81.0
20. Tampa	75.9	20. Dallas/Ft. Worth	80.9
21. Newark	75.3	21. Salt Lake City	80.1
22. Seattle	75.0	22. Detroit	78.8
23. Atlanta	74.6	23. St. Louis	78.2
24. Boston	74.3	24. Chicago O'Hare	78.1
25. New York Kennedy	73.1	25. San Francisco	78.1
26. San Francisco	71.2	26. Atlanta	77.6
27. Los Angeles	70.8	27. Los Angeles	77.4
Average On-Time Arrivals	*78.0*	*Average On-Time Departures*	*81.0*

"Let's Go Feel!"

I am a traveler, not a tourist. Whenever I travel to old favorites or explore new destinations, I try to "feel" as much as possible the people, the land, the culture, the sights, the sounds, the smells, and the cuisine of where I am visiting. As an outsider, it is not possible to "feel" as the locals might, but I do the best I can. As I have walked the streets of Bombay and bicycled through the rural villages of India, passed through small villages in the Andes Mountains of South America, visited nomadic tribes in the Arabian deserts, and sailed through the remote Vava'u Islands of the South Pacific, I cannot fully connect with the struggle of daily life, but I try and am richly rewarded for my efforts. I always try to learn a few phrases in the native language of the countries I visit. The natives know I do not speak their language, but they seem to appreciate my effort and my rough-hewn attempts to communicate always bring smiles.

On one of my journeys to Australia, I lived with an Aboriginal family deep in the Outback. I lived as they lived—hunted with them, ate with them, did everything they did. It was one of the most rewarding experiences of my life; and yet, I knew that in three weeks I would be back in Sydney and then home to America.

In Samoa, I stay with a family in the village of Matareva. The Saili family live a traditional lifestyle without modern conveniences, except for a single bulb hanging in the middle of their open sided fale. Many families in the village have no electricity whatsoever. No beds, except the floor; no refrigerator; all water is fetched from a nearby stream; food is gathered daily and all meals are cooked over an open fire. Life is good, but hard. I stay with my friends in their village, but I knew in the not far distant I would be boarding a flight that would take me elsewhere. This scene has been repeated for me all over the world. Knowing that I am an invited observer and not a permanent fixture colors my vision.

I remember visiting Russia not long after the break-up of the Soviet Union. I enjoy Russia; I really do. A proud people and proud country broken by an evil system. I was always struck by the dour expression on the faces of most Russians. "Why are you so unhappy? You have overthrown the shackles of Communism."

Life is hard in Russia. Very, very hard. Private apartments are rare and virtually out of reach for common folks. The Russian ruble has little constant value. (Everyone wants "greenbacks".) Food is sometimes scarce. Crime is increasing. Both parents work and still they cannot make ends meet. Life is not romantic and, by and large, is not fun.

Cathy and I were in St. Petersburg. Our excursion this day took us to the Peterhof Palace of Petrodvorets, the royal summer residence and palace of the czars built by Peter the Great. The palace, some 19 miles west of St. Petersburg, is a remarkable and stunning architectural wonder. The Grand Cascade is one of the most impressive fountains in the world. The 30 acre estate is dotted with sculptures, flower gardens, and lush wooded areas. I could "feel" the czarist social life in the Throne Room, Portrait Room, and ascending the ornate Grand Staircase. Yet something was missing. The palace was beautiful, but still, the experience was lacking. There was an emptiness and despair. A feeling of hopelessness. We attended church services at a small rural Russian Orthodox Church and I still felt a hunger of the human spirit.

I asked our guide Olga, "Why does no one smile? It seems no one is happy?"

Her reply was quick and to the point, "What is their to be happy about?" Our conversation left the history of czarist Russia and focused on the daily grind of life that Russian people face. Olga asked, "What is there to hope for?" The opportunities of entrepreneurship are bogged down in endless bureaucracy and corruption. I thought to myself, "It will take two or three generations to revitalize the Russian spirit." I guess it is true that one doesn't put new wine in old bottles.

Later that week we spent the day touring the monuments, sights, and city of St. Petersburg, founded by Czar Peter the Great in 1703. The city was meant to symbolize the Europeanization of Russia, and no expense was spared in making it one of the most beautiful cities in the world. Today the city has more than 50 museums and 20 theatres and concert halls. Palaces and gardens abound throughout the city.

One of the most impressive sites is the Hermitage or Winter Palace, a complex of five buildings founded by Catherine the Great in 1764 along the Neva River. This former royal palace houses close to one million works of art, including important Renaissance paintings. Paintings by Da Vinci, Rembrandt, Rubens, and Titian are displayed here. We visited the Aurora, the battleship that fired the shot signaling the storming of the Winter Palace by the Bolsheviks in 1917; the Peter and Paul Fortress, which houses the tomb of Peter the Great; Palace Square with the Alexander Monument commemorating the victory over Napoleon; and, of course, St. Isaac's Cathedral.

Our guide for the next few days was Ludmila, a middle-aged woman who seemed to know everything. She was obsessed that we see every building, monument, cathedral, and shop in the city. I was grateful for her efficiency and knowledge. We found ourselves, one day, with an afternoon to spare. Ludmila suggested several shopping areas along Nevsky Prospekt, St. Petersburg's main street and shopping area. And, of course, there were a few museums we had not yet seen.

Surprisingly, Ludmila asked us what we wanted to do. (I had become accustomed in Russia to being told what I would do and see.) I told her I wanted to get away from the shops and experience everyday Russian life. I told her I wanted to "feel" the city and her people. Ludmila looked at me as though I had lost my mind. I knew what she was thinking, "Why would you come so far from America to visit the streets, back alleys, markets, and hassles of Russia?" She did not seem to understand my need to "feel," but then how could she? Life for her is a daily struggle with seemingly little hope for tomorrow. To her I probably live the life of a czar.

She again suggested several museums and foreign tourist shops. I said, "No. Ludmila, I really want to see life as you do, experience what it is to live as Russians do. I want to *do* what everyday Russians do. I want to *feel* Russian life." Another strange look and then she said with a forward wave of her arm, "Okay, let's go *feel!*"

We spent the balance of the day away from the tourist areas and went into the heart and soul of St. Petersburg. Long lines were everywhere and for everything. Ludmila shook her head when I told her I wanted to stand in line for bread. First, I stood in a "snake" line that went out the door and down the street. Now, *this* is a long, long line. Finally I got to the front. Did I get my loaf of bread? No! The first line was to *pay* for the bread, a second line to get the bread. Out the door I went again. I got strange looks from the others waiting in line. Who is this American? Why does he come to Russia to stand in line for bread? When my turn came, I handed the clerk my receipt and received my loaf of fresh Russian bread. Ludmila was now convinced I was crazy. I loved it! It was the experience I wanted, not the bread.

We walked through an unmarked, back alley to a small square known to locals as "Stroganoff Square," reportedly where the beef dish originated. As we approached this private area, a guard, thinking we were Russian (now, that's a stretch isn't it?), barked at us telling us to get lost. Ludmila explained we were visitors from America and just seeing the sights today. His expression and demeanor changed instantly. "Welcome! Please come in. I have a cousin in New York City. Do you know him?" he asked and Ludmila translated. "Sorry, I haven't had the pleasure of meeting your cousin," I answered.

Want to "feel" Russian life? Literally? We climbed on a city bus that was so crowded and tightly packed (tourists *never* see this stuff, travelers do) that I couldn't even raise my arm to scratch my nose. We rode the subway, walked the streets, shopped in the open markets, and didn't see many tourists. "Beware of pick pockets," Ludmila warned. "They are everywhere!" I kept my wallet in my front pocket with my hand on it.

I asked to visit a food store. No Safeways here. The store measured about 40 feet by 15 feet. It was typical of food stores everywhere in Russia. One does not walk up and down the isles putting food items in a basket. Canned goods are behind the counter. If there is any meat, it sits in a cooler. On the day we visited, no beef or sausage was available. Canned goods were scarce. There were a few wrapped packages of chicken parts. ("Parts" is the best term to describe it.) That was it.

We had been looking for a bottle of Pepsi with all Russian writing on it. We had been told that the new Pepsi bottles would be labeled in English. We wanted the "real thing." We had looked all day, but no luck. Ludmila asked if any Pepsi was available. None. We then asked Ludmila to ask the shop keeper if there were any *empty* Pepsi bottles we could buy. Speaking in Russian, the shop keeper said disgustingly, "They're crazy! Why would anyone want to buy an empty bottle?" Well, we bought our empty bottles with all Russian writing on them.

I asked Ludmila about a particular store that sold military equipment and uniforms. I thought it would be fun to take something home. Her reply came quickly, "You cannot go there!"

"Why?" (In Russia one does not ask "why?")

"Because the store is only for those in the military. You must have official papers to buy anything."

Now, I know something about capitalism and the value of "greenbacks" [U.S. dollars] in Russia. "Ludmila, please just take me there." After several more protests from Ludmila, she saw that I was determined to get myself into trouble and figured it was better for me to go with her than do it alone.

We made our way to the store. I wanted to take home a hat or something. I asked Ludmila to tell the clerk what I wanted and that I would pay in U.S. dollars. She told me to stand where I was. She walked across the store and spoke with the clerk. His head jerked up, his eyes widened, and he looked me over intently.

After a few more minutes of back and forth, Ludmila walked over to me and said, "He will go through the door behind the counter. Wait a moment and then you follow him in."

"Ludmila, I want you to come in with me."

"No. He speaks good English. I cannot go in there."

"Ludmila, come with me. You wait for me to go in and then come in behind me."

I looked at the clerk and gave a slight nod. He opened the door to the mysterious back room and disappeared. I walked behind the counter, past a big sign that said in Russian, "Official orders required for purchase." Ludmila was not far behind me. After disappearing behind the door, would I ever be seen again? Would I disappear and end up in some *gulag* in Siberia?

What a sight! A long room with hundreds of military uniforms, medals, hats, belts, and equipment. Anything and everything the well dressed Russian GI would need!

"Vhat do you vant to buy?"

"An officer's hat and anything else that's interesting."

"You pay in Ah-meri-can doll-ers?"

"Yes." With 'that affirmative answer, a large table was filled for me to choose from. Officers' dress hats, watches, medals, belts, pants, jackets, uniforms, fur caps,....you name it, it was on the table.

"You vant a general's uni-form?" The man pulled out a complete uniform with a general's designation. There were pants, shirt, tie, boots, jacket, overcoat, and hat, and my pick of medals. I could see myself standing on a balconey in Red Square with the other big shots at the May Day Parade!

"No, I think I'll take these." I picked out two officer hats, a fur cap with a hammer and sickle (I gave it to my teenage son to wear skiing), a belt buckle, several medals, and a official KGB watch. (I tried talking into the watch to see if there were any secret codes, but no luck!)

I assumed we would bargain on the cost. "How much do you want for this," pointing to the officer's hat?

"Thû-ree doll-ers."

I could tell he expected a counter offer from me, but for three dollars I couldn't bring myself to whittle the price down. I left the shop with a large sack of hats, belts, watches, caps, and medals for about $20. Ludmila shook her head.

What an exciting afternoon! I experienced Russian life as best I could. The best part of the tour was when Ludmila waved her arm and said, "Okay, let's go feel!"

Epilogue

Saving money on your travel is more an attitude than anything else. It is taking control of your situation. The best advice for saving on your travel is plan ahead, be flexible, and find a street smart travel guy to keep a constant flow of information coming your way. Knowledge is power! Knowledge gives you the power to make informed decisions. Knowledge is the power to have options that most of the traveling public doesn't have because they don't know. And what they don't know will hurt them right where it really hurts! In the wallet!

Travel is a dynamic industry that is in a constant state of change. What is available today and what works today may not be here tomorrow. The only edge you have is information. Position yourself in the middle of the travel information highway. Make sure you are receiving the constant flow of new travel bargains, offers, discounts, options, and savings. Let the guy sitting next to you pay the regular rate. You go for free or at a fraction of his cost!

Happy sailing! And stay tuned for Volume 2.

Airline Frequent Flyer Programs With Airline, Hotel, And Car Rental Participating Partners

The information listed below is current as of the printing date and is subject to change without notice by the airlines, hotels, and car rental companies involved. Participating partners are travel suppliers on which you can earn frequent flyer credit. For example, if you are an American Airlines AAdvantage Program member, you can earn frequent flyer credit each time you fly American, and you can also earn AAdvantage credit when you rent a car from Alamo or stay at a Holiday Inn Hotel. Most airlines have many participating partners. The two letter airline code is listed after the carrier.

Information and enrollment is available for the telephone and fax numbers listed with each airline. You may also enroll at any airport or city ticket office of each respective airline. Information is provided only for airlines that fly in and out of the United States.

Aer Lingus (EI) *Travel Award Bonus*

Tel:	212-557-1090, or any Aer Lingus airport or ticket office
Airlines:	Aer Lingus
Car Rentals:	Avis, Europcar Interrent, Hertz
Hotels:	Jurys Hotel Group Ireland

Aerolineas Argentinas (AR) *Aerolineas Plus*

Airlines:	Aerolineas Argentinas, Austral, Aviaco, Binter Canarias, Binter, Mediterraneo, Iberia, Viasa, Viva Air
Car Rentals:	Avis, Hertz
Hotels:	Inter·Continental, Occidental Hotels, Melia Hotels, Sol Hotels

Aeromexico (AM) *Club Premier*

Tel:	800-247-3737
Fax:	713-939-7242
Airlines:	Aeromexico, Aerolitoral, Aeromar, AeroPoniente, Aeroperu, Air France, America West, British Airways, Delta, Mexicana
Car Rentals:	Avis, Budget
Hotels:	Crowne Plaza (Mexico), Fiesta Americana (Mexico), Fiesta Inn (Mexico), Holiday Inn (Mexico), Hyatt Hotels International, Inter-Continental Hotels, Radisson International

Aeroperu (PL) *Club Premier*

Tel:	800-777-7717
Fax:	305-591-9240
Airlines:	Aerolitoral, Aeromar, Aeromexico, Aeroperu, Air France, Air LA, America West, British Airways, Japan Airlines, Mexicana (international)
Car Rentals:	Avis, Budget
Hotels:	Crowne Plaza (Mexico), Fiesta Americana (Mexico), Fiesta Inn (Mexico), Holiday Inn (Mexico), Radisson International
Other:	American Express Member Miles, High Life Department Stores (Mexico)

Air Canada (AC) *Aeroplan.*

Tel:	800-361-8253	USA
	800-361-5373	Canada
Fax:	514-395-2496	
Airlines:	Air Alliance, AirBC, Air Canada, Air Creebac, Air Nova, Air Ontario, Austrian Airlines, Bearskin Airlines, Cathay Pacific, Continental, Finnair, First Air, Interprovincal, NWT Air, Swissair, United Airlines	
Car Rentals:	Avis, Budget, Hertz	
Hotels:	Hilton International, Hilton Hotels & Resorts, Holiday Inn, Hotel Des Gouverneurs, Sheraton, Keddy's Hotels & Inns, Marriott Hotels, Resorts & Suites, Ocean Pointe Resort, Radisson International, Regina Inn, The Charlottetown, Westin Hotels & Resorts	
Other:	Air Canada Vacation, AGT, Bell Canada, BC Tel, CICB Aerogold VISA, Diners Club/enRoute, Island Tel, MT&T, MTS, Newfoundland Telephone, NBTel, Park'N Fly, Sasktel, Unitel	

Air France (AF) *Frequence Plus*
Tel: 800-237-2747
Airlines: Aeromexico, Air France, Air Inter Europe, Britair,
                Eurowings, Japan Airlines
Car Rentals: Avis, Hertz
Hotels: Le Meridien, Forte Grand, Sheraton
Other: American Express (France, Germany, Holland, Italy,
                Spain, Sweden, Switzerland, UK, Argentina), Callway,
                Disneyland Paris, Jet Tours, France Telecom, Global One
                (Deutsche Telekom, France Telecom, Sprint)

Alaska Airlines (AS) *Mileage Plan*
Tel: 800-654-5669   Service Center
                800-426-0333   Reservations
Fax: 206-433-3477
Airlines: Alaska Airlines, Bering Air, British Airways, ERA,
                Horizon, LAB FlyingServices (flight credit only),
                Northwest, PenAir, Qantas, Reeve Aleutian Airways,
                SAS, TWA
Can Rentals: Alamo, Budget, Hertz
Hotels: Coast Hotels - Canada, Hilton Hotels, Holiday Inn, Hyatt
                Hotels & Resorts, Kimpton Hotels, Preferred Hotels,
                Princess Cruise Hotels, Red Lion, West Coast Hotels,
                Westin, Westmark
Other: Seafirst VISA and MasterCard, Diners Club, ALAS
                COM, Flower Club

Alitalia (AZ) *Premium Program MileMiglia ITA Members*
Tel: 800-223-5730
Airlines: Alitalia, British Midland, Continental, Malev
Car Rentals: Hertz
Hotels: Sheraton Club International

All Nippon Airways (NH) *Program A*
Tel: 800-262-4653
Airlines: All Nippon, Austrian, Delta, Swissair, USAir.
Hotels: ANA Hotels, Swissotels

Aloha Airlines (AQ) *AlohaPass Travel Award Program*
Tel: 800-367-5250   outside Hawaii
                808-486-7277   Hawaii
Airlines: Aloha Airlines, Island Air

Car Rentals:	Budget (Hawaii awards only), Dollar
Hotels:	Selected Aston Hotels & Resorts, Colony Hotels, Executive Centre, Hilton Waikoloa Village, Outrigger Hotels Hawaii, Ritz Carlton Kapalua, Ritz Carlton Mauna Lani (awards only), Sheraton Hotels Hawaii
Others:	Atlantis Submarines, Royal Hawaain Cruises, Kapalua Villas Hotels/Golf package, Kauai Lagoons, Waliea Gold Golf Course

America West Airlines. (HP) *FlightFund*

Tel:	800-247-5691 Service Center
	800-235-9292 Reservations
Airlines:	Aeromexico, Air France (award partner only), Air New Zealand, America West Express, British Airways, Continental, Northwest (award partner only), Sun Trips (award partner only)
Car Rentals:	Alamo, Avis, Dollar, Thirfty
Hotels:	Crowne Plaza, Hilton & Conrad International Center, Holiday Inn Westin
Other:	*FlightFund* VISA Card (Bank of America), Sprint

American Airlines. (AA) *AAdvantage Program*

Tel:	800-882-8880 Service Center
	800-433-7300 Domestic Reservations
	800-624-6262 International Reservations
Fax:	817-963-7702
Airlines:	American, American Eagle, British Airways (award travel only), British Midland (award travel only), Canadian Airlines International, Cathay Pacific, Hawaiian, Japan, Midway, Midway Connection, Qantas, Reno Air, Singapore, South African Airways
Can Rentals:	Alamo, Avis, Hertz, National, Interrent
Hotels:	Conrad International, Crowne Plaza, Fairmont, Fiesta Americana/Fiesta Inn, Forte, Forum, Hilton, Holiday Inn, Hyatt, Inter-Continental, Sheraton, Le Meridien, Loews, Marriott, Red Lion, Sandals, Vista, Westin, Wyndham.
Other:	AAdvantage Dining, American AAdvantage Funds, AAdvantage Incentive Miles, Citibank AAdvantage MasterCard or VISA, MCI Long Distance, SNET MobilCom, 1-800-SEND FTD

Asiana Airlines (OZ) *Asiana Bonus Club - Americas*

Tel: 213-365-4516
Fax: 213-380-1688
Airlines: Asiana, Northwest, Northwest Airlink
Car Rentals: Hertz (Korea), National/Nippon Interrent
Hotels: Holiday Inn, Radisson, Westin, Oxford, Palace Hotel
                (Los Angeles)

Austrian Airlines (OS) *Qualiflyer*
Swissair (SR) *Qualiflyer*

Tel: 800-221-8125
Fax: 718-670-8619
Airlines: Air Canada, All Nippon Airways, Ansett Australia,
                Austrian, Austrian Airtransport, Cathay Pacific, Crossair,
                Delta, Malaysia, Sabena, Singapore, Swissair, Tyrolean
Car Rentals: Avis, Europcar Interrent, Hertz
Hotels: ANA International, Hilton International, Inter·
                Continental, Swissotel
Other: Airplus (Austria), Eurocard-MasterCard (Switzerland),
                Amexco (Argentina, Belgium, Brazil, France, Germany,
                Israel, Italy, Netherlands, South Africa, Spain,
                Switzerland, U.K., U.S.A.), Diners Club (Austria,
                Israel, Switzerland)

Avianca Airlines (AV) *Sociedad Aeronautico De Medallian (MM)*
Avianca Plus

Tel: 800-284-1758
Airlines: Avianca, Latin Pass (ACES, Aviateca, COPA, Faucett,
                LACSA, Lloyd Aereo Boliviano, Lan Chile, LADECO,
                NICA, SAETA, Taca, TransBrazil, USAir), Mexicana,
                Sociedad Aeronautico de Medallian (SAM)
Car Rentals: Avis, Hertz
Other: Bancoquia-VISA (Columbia residents), Espectador
                Newspaper (residents of Santa Fe de Bogota, Medellin,
                Cali Barranquilla, Bucaramanga, Ibaque, Caragena,
                Valledupar, Tunja, Nieva, Eoirardot, Quibdo), Sprint
                Foncard

British Airways (BA) *Executive Club - USA Programme*

Tel: 800-955-2748
Airlines: Aeromexico, Alaska/Horizon, American (award travel
                only), British Airways, Qantas, USAir, USAir Express,

	USAir Shuttle
Car Rentals:	Alamo, Hertz
Hotels:	Hilton, Hilton International, Mandarin Orient Group, Marriott, Radisson Edwardian London, Radisson Worldwide, Ritz-Carlton, Savoy Group, Southern Sun, Taj Group
Other:	AT&T, Camelot Chauffer Drive, Chase/British Airways VISA card, Diners Club, The Flower Group, Travelex Foreign Currency Services

Canadian Airlines International (CP) *Canadian Plus*

Tel:	800-426-7000	USA
	800-663-0290	Canada
Fax:	604-270-5476	
Airlines:	Air Alma, Air Atlantic, Air Labrador, Air New Zealand (participating routes only), Aloha Airlines, Aloha IslandAir, American, American Eagle, Calm Air, Canadian Airlines International, Canadian North, Canadian Regional, Inter-Canadien, Lufthansa, North-Wright Air, Pem-Air, Ptarmigan Airways, Qantas (participating routes only)	
Can Rentals:	Europcar Interrent, National, Thrifty, Tilden	
Hotels:	Albatross Motel-Gander NF, Cambridge Suites-Sydney NS, Explorer Hotel Yellowknife NWT, Gateway Hotel Toronto, Glynmill Inn-Corner Brook NF, participating Canadian Pacific Hotels, Coast, Delta, Evaz Group, Forum, Inter·Continental, Prince, Ramada, Renaissance International, Shangri-La, Westcoast, Westmark	
Other:	AMJ Atlas Van Lines, Brewster Transportation & Tours Canadian Holidays, Aeropark, Flowers, 24 Hours, Park & Jet, Stentor Alliance of Canada, YVR Par	

Carnival Air Lines (KW) *FunPass*

Tel:	954-923-0406
Airlines:	Carnival

Cathay Pacific (CX) *Passages Frequent Flyer Programme.*
Malaysia Airlines (MH) *Passages Frequent Flyer Programme*
Singapore Airlines (SQ) *Passages Frequent Flyer Programme*
For enrollment ands information, contact any of the three airlines

Airlines:	All Nippon, Austrian, British Airways, Cathay Pacific, Delta, Malaysia, Sabena, SilkAir, Singapore, Swissair

Car Rentals:	Avis, Hertz
Hotels:	Hilton International, Hyatt, Inter·Continental, Sheraton, Mandarin Oriental, Group, Pan Pacific, Regent International, Shangri-La
Other:	American Express, Citibank VISA/MasterCard, Diners Club, Singapore Telecom, Islobal One

China Airlines (CI) *Dynasty Flyer Program*
Mandarin Airlines (AE) *Dynasty Flyer Program*

Tel:	800-227-5118 ext. 5
Airlines:	China, Continental, Mandarin
Hotels:	Mandarin Oriental Group, Regal International
Other:	American Express Membership Miles, Utell International

Continental Airlines (CO) *OnePass*

Tel:	713-952-1630 INFOPASS
	800-344-1411 Award travel
	800-344-3333 Partners travel
	800-525-0280 Domestic reservations
	800-231-0856 International reservations
Airlines:	Aer Lingus, Aerolineas Argentinas, Air Canada, Alitalia, America West, BWIA, Continental, Continental Express, Continental Micronesia, CSA Czech, Iberia, Lan Chile, Malaysia, Qantas, SAS, Sky West
Car Rentals:	Dollar, EuroDollar, Europcar, National Interrent, Thrifty, Tilden
Hotels:	Aston, Camino Real, Conrad International, Fiesta Americana, Fiesta Inn, Hilton USA, Sheraton, Marriott, Melia and Sol, Radisson
Other:	American Express Membership Miles, Diners Club, Marine Midland Gold MasterCard, MasterCard, VISA

Delta Air Lines (DL) *SkyMiles*

Tel:	800-323-2323 Service Center
	800-221-1212 Domestic reservations
	800-241-4141 International reservations
Airlines:	Air New Zealand, Aer Lingus, Aeromexico, All Nippon, Atlantic Southeast, Austrian, Business Express, Comair, Delta, Sabena, Singapore, SkyWest, Swissair, VARIG
Car Rentals:	Alamo, Avis, Hertz
Hotels:	Crowne Plaza, Forte, Hilton Conrad, Hilton

International, Holiday Inn, Hyatt, Inter·Continental & Forum, Sheraton, Le Meredien, Marriott, Preferred, Radisson, Swissotel.

Other:	American Express Membership Miles, AT&T True Rewards, Diners Club, Renaissance Cruise Lines, The Flower Club

El Al Israel Airlines (LY) *Frequent Flyer Club - Matmid*

Tel:	800-223-6700 or 212-852,0604
Airlines:	El Al
Fee:	$35 membership fee

Eva Airways (BR) *Evergreen Club*

For enrollment and information, contact Eva Airways

Airlines:	Eva Airways

Finnair (AY) *Finnair Plus Frequent Traveler Plan*

For enrollment and information, contact Finnair

Airlines:	Delta, Finnair, Lufthansa
Car Rentals:	Avis, Europcar Interrent, Hertz
Hotels:	Arctic Hotels Partners (except in Helsinki), Inter·Continental (Helsinki), Gateway Hotel (Helsinki), Gothenburg and Malmo Scandic, Hotel Strand Inter-Continental (Helsinki), Savoy Hotel (Moscow)
Other:	Silja Line Cruise Ships

Hawaiian Airlines (HA) *Gold Plus*

Tel:	800-367-7637
Fax:	808-536-6960
Airlines:	Hawaiian, Northwest
Car Rentals:	Alamo, Avis
Hotels:	Aston, Castle, Hawaiian Pacific, Village Resorts
Other:	Pahio Vacations, Schuler Homes, Windjammer Cruises

Iberia - Lineas Aereas de Espana (IB) *Iberia Plus - North America*

Tel:	800-772-4642 or 305-267-7747
Airlines:	Aerolineas Argentinas, Austral, Aviaco, Binter Canarias, Binter Mediterraneo, Iberia, Regional, Viasa, Viva
Car Rentals:	Avis, Hertz
Hotels:	Forum, Inter·Continental, Melia, Occidental, Sol

Japan Airlines (JL) *JAL Mileage Bank - Americas*
Tel: 800-525-6453
Airlines: Aeromexico, Aeroperu, Air France, American, Japan,
                Japan Asia Airways

KLM Royal Dutch Airlines (KL) *Flying Dutchman "World of Difference"*
Tel: 800-374-7747
Airlines: Air UK, KLM, KLM Cityhopper, Northwest, Transavia
Car Rentals: Avis
Hotels: Golden Tulip, Holiday Inn, Inter·Continental & Forum,
                Sheraton

Korean Air (KE) *Skypass*
Tel: 800-525-4480 or 213-484-5780
Fax: 213-484-5790
Airlines: Korean Air
Hotels: Omni Los Angeles, Sheraton Anchorage, Waikiki Resort
                (Honolulu), KAL Hotels, Cheju and Seo Kwi Po on
                Cheju Island

LACSA - Lineas Aereas Costarricenses S.A. (LR) *LACSAPass*
Tel: 800-225-2272 or 506-232-9876
Fax: 506-231-0558
Airlines: Aviateca, COPA, LACSA, NICA, TACA

LanChile Airlines (LA) *LanPass*
Tel: 800-735-5526
Airlines: LanChile

LOT Polish Airlines (LO) *Frequent Flyer Program*
Tel: 800-223-0593
Airlines: ·LOT Polish Airlines
Car Rentals: Avis, Hertz
Hotels: Inter·Continental, Orbis (Poland)

Lufthansa German Airlines (LH) *Lufthansa Miles & More*
Tel: 800-581-6400
Fax: 516-296-9474
Airlines: Air Dolomiti, Air Canada, Adria Airways (selected
                routes), British Midland, Business Air, Finnair (selected
                routes), Lauda Air, Lufthansa, Luxair (selected flights),
                Thai International, SAS, South African, Tyrolean

	(selected flights), United, United Express, Varig
Car Rentals:	Avis, Budget, Hertz, Sixt
Hotels:	Forum, Hilton International (excluding Hilton USA and Hilton National UK), Holiday Inn (excluding Holiday Inn Express), Inter•Continental, Sheraton (excluding USA and Canada), ITT Sheraton Luxury Collection (USA), Kempinski, Marriott, Ramada International (excluding USA and Canada), Renaissance, Vista (USA)
Others:	BMW MgmbH, Condor, Disneyland Paris, "Pilot for a Day" LH Airline Training Center, LH Taditionsflug GmbH, LSG Lufthansa Service, Lufthansa Simulator, Sun Express

Malaysian Airlines. *Passages Frequent Flyer Programme*
See Cathay Pacific Airlines

Mexicana Airlines (MX) *Frecuentra*

Tel:	800-531-7901
Airlines:	Aeroliteral, Aeromar, Aeromexico, Latin Pass (ACES Avianca, Aviateca, COPA, Faucett, LACSA, Laderco, Lloyd Aereo Boliviano, LanChile, NICA, SEATA, TACA, Transbrasil, USAir), Mexicana
Car Rentals:	Avis, Executive (Mexico)
Hotels:	Camino Real, El Cid Mega, Fiesta Americana, Fiesta Inn, Maeva, Paraiso Radisson, Presidente Inter•Continental, Sierra Radisson, Westin, Hilton (USA), Radisson International (USA)
Other:	American Express Membership Miles, Diners Club, Frecuentra/BITAL/MasterCard, Frecuentra Sprint Phonecard

Midwest Express (YX) *Frequent Flyer*

Tel:	800-452-2022 Service Center
	800-452-2022 Reservations
Fax:	414-570-0192
Airlines:	Air New Zealand, Northwest, Swissair, Skyway, Virgin Atlantic
Car Rentals:	Alamo, Avis, Hertz, National Interrent
Hotels:	The American Club-Kohler, Hilton, Pfister Hotel-Milwaukee, Wyndham

NICA (6Y) *NICAPASS*
Tel: 800-831-6422 or 305-223-0312
Fax: 305-223-1731
Airlines: APA, BWIA, Latin Pass (ACES, Avianca, Aviateca,
                COPA, Faucett, LACSA, Ladeco, Lloyd Aereo
                Boliviano, LanChile, Mexicana, SAETA, TACA,
                Transbrasil, USAir), LAPSA, NICA
Car Rentals: Avis

Northwest Airlines (NW) *WorldPerks*
Tel: 800-447-3757 Service Center and Award Reservations
                800-327-2881 Automated Mileage Information
                800-225-2525 Reservations
Airlines: Air New Zealand, Air UK, Alaska, America West,
                Asiana, Eurowing, Hawaiian, Horizon Air, KLM,
                Northwest, Northwest Airlink, Pacific Island Aviation,
                Royal Dutch
Car Rentals: Alamo, Avis, Hertz, National Interrent
Hotels: Conrad International, Courtyard by Marriott, Crowne
                Plaza, Fairfield by Marriott, Hilton (USA), Holiday Inn,
                Hyatt, Golden Tulip, Sheraton, Marriott, New Otani,
                Peabody, Radisson, Shangri-La, Tulip Inns, Westin.
Others: MCI Long Distance & Paging Services, Flower Club

Qantas (QF) *Qantas Australian Frequent Flyer Program*
Tel: 800-227-4500
Airlines: American, Austrian Airlink, Australia, Asia, Air Pacific,
                British Airways, Canadian International, Eastern
                Australia, National Jet Systems, Qantas, SAS, Southern
                Australia, Sunstate, USAir
Car Rentals: Hertz, Thrifty
Fee: $30 one-time membership fee

Sabena Belgian World Airlines (SN) *Sabena Frequent Flyer Programme.*
Tel: 800-955-2000
Airlines: Austrian, Sabena, Swissair
Car Rentals: Avis
Hotels: Hilton International, Holiday Inn, Sabena
Other: Ceran Lingua, Diners Club (Belgium and Luxembourg
                residents), Jet Tours

Scandinavian Airlines Systems (SK) *SAS EuroBonus*

Tel:	800-221-2350
Airlines:	Air Baltic (between Riga and Copenhagen, Helsinki, or Stockholm), Air New Zealand (excluding flights to/from Europe plus between Bangkok and Sydney), British Midland, Continental, Icelandair (between Reykjavik and Copenhagen, Oslo, Stockholm, and between Copenhagen and Hamburg), Lufthansa (excluding flights between Germany and Finland), Qantas (excluding flights to/from Europe), SAS, Thai International (excluding flights between Paris and Stockholm), United
Car Rentals:	Avis, Hertz
Hotels:	Forum, Inter·Continental, Radisson SAS, Swissotel

Singapore Airlines *Passages Frequent Flyer Programme*
   See Cathay Pacific Airlines

South African Airways *Voyager*

Tel:	800-722-9675
Airlines:	Alliance, American, Ansett Australia, British Midland, Lufthansa, SA Airlink, SA Express, Thai International
Car Rentals:	Avis, Budget, Imperial
Hotels:	Holiday Inn, Hyatt, Inter·Continental, Forum, Kempinski, Southern Sun Group (South Africa)
Other:	Cunard Cruises, Diners Club, Global One, Mobile Telephone Networks (MTN), Nedbank, Rennies Foreign Exchange

Southwest Airlines (WN) *Rapid Rewards*

Tel:	800-445-9267 Service Center
	800-435-9792 Reservations
Airlines:	Southwest
Car Rentals:	Alamo, Budget, Hertz
Other:	American Express Membership Miles, Diners Club, MCI

TAP Air Portugal (TP) *Programa Passageiro Frequenta*

Tel:	800-221-7370
Airlines:	TAP Air Portugal
Car Rentals:	Avis
Hotels:	Meridien, Occidental

Thai Airways International (TG) *Royal Orchid Plus*
Tel: 800-426-5204
Airlines: Ansett Australia, Lufthansa, Thai International, SAS,
South African, United
Hotels: Accor Asia-Pacific, Amari, Dusit, Holiday Inn, Sheraton,
Kempinski, Marriott, Royal Garden, Royal Princess

Turkish Airlines (TK) *Turk Hava Yollari Frequent Flyer Mileage Club*
Tel: 800-874-8875
Airlines: Turkish

Trans World Airlines (TW) *Frequent Flight Bonus*
Tel: 800-325-4815 Service Center
800-221-2000 Domestic reservations
800-892-4141 International reservations
Fax: 610-631-5280
Airlines: Aerolineas Argentinas, Air India, Alaska, Philippine,
TWA, TWA Express
Car Rentals: Alamo, Avis, Thrifty
Hotels: Adam's Mark, Conrad International, Forte, Hilton, Inter-
Continental, Marriott, Radisson, Renaissance
Other: Affinity Card-EAB, Flower Club, LDDS World
Com*Sprint Communications, TWA Getaway Card,
TWA Getaway Vacations

United Airlines (UA) *Mileage Plus*
Tel: 800-421-4655 or 605-399-2400   Service Center
800-241-6522   Domestic reservations
800-538-2929   International reservations
Airlines: Aeromar, Air Canada, Air France, ALM Antillean, Aloha,
Ansett Australian, British Midland, Gulf Stream
International, LAPA (Argentina), Lufthansa, National
Airlines Chile S.A., SAS, Thai International, Shuttle by
United, United, United Express
Car Rentals: Alamo, Avis, Budget, Hertz, National Interrent.
Hotels: Demeure and Libertel, Grupo Sol, Grupo Sol Melia,
Hilton, Hilton International, Holiday Inn, Hyatt, Inter-
Continental, Marriott, Radisson, Shagri-La, Sheraton,
Ritz Carlton, Vista, Westin
Other: AT&T, Crystal Cruises, Norwegian Cruise Line,
Renaissance Cruises, Royal Cruise Lines

Frequent Lodging Programs

Please note that the information listed is correct as of the date of printing. Programs, details, terms, conditions, awards, and telephone numbers are subject to change without notice by the sponsoring hotel.

AmeriSuites	*AmeriClub*	404-955-9007
Best Western	*Gold Crown Club International*	800-237-8483
ClubHouse Inns	*BestGuest*	800-CLUB-INN (258-2466)
Courtyard by Marriott	*Courtyard Club Award*	800-321-7396
Crowne Plaza Hotels & Resorts	*Crown Plaza Preferred*	800-272-9273
Days Inn	*The Inn-Credible Card*	800-547-7878
Fairfield Inn by Marriott	*INNsiders Club*	800-443-7200
The Fairmont Hotels	*The President's Club*	800-522-3437
Hilton and Conrad Hilton Hotels	*Hilton Honors*	800-HILTONS (445-8667)
Holiday Inn	*Priority Club*	800-272-9273

Hyatt Hotels.	*Gold Passport*	800-54-HYATT (544-9288)
Inter·Continental Hotels & Resorts	*Six Continents Club*	800-327-0200
ITT Sheraton Hotels and Resorts	*Sheraton Club International (SCI)*	919-876-9259
La Quinta Inns	*Returns Club*	800-531-5900
Marriott Hotels, Resorts & Suites	*Marriott Honored Guests Awards*	800-367-6453
Ramada Franchise Systems, Inc.	*Ramada Business Card*	800-672-6232
Red Lion Hotels	*Frequent Guest Dividends Program*	*800-547-8010*
Renaissance Hotels & Resorts	*Club Express Program*	800-468-3571
Travelodge	*Club Express Program*	Information is available at any Travelodge
Westin Hotels & Resorts	*Westin Premier*	800-228-3000
Wyndham Hotels & Resorts	*Frequent Guest Program*	214-978-4500

Tourist And Visitor Information Offices

One of the best and most overlooked sources of travel destination information is tourist and visitor bureaus. Their purpose is to provide information, maps, guides and recommendations to visitors. Always ask if any discount coupon books are available.

Listed below are tourist board offices for each state, a selection of popular cities, counties, and foreign destinations. The list of cities, counties, and overseas locations is not intended to be exhaustive, but includes the most popular destinations.

If the listing you want for a United States destination is not provided, call 800-555-1212 and ask if there is a toll-free number for a tourist board for your desired destination. Or, call information for the city or area you are desiring and ask for the tourist board, visitors office, or convention bureau. Call the desired area code, followed by 555-1212. You can get the applicable area code from your telephone directory.

If your international tourist board is not listed here, it is a safe bet that they maintain an office in New York City or Los Angeles. Call the information directory for New York City or Los Angeles and ask for the telephone number for that country's tourism office.

Ask for a copy of *The Convention & Visitors Bureau Telephone Directory* from the International Association of Convention & Visitors Bureau, P.O. Box 6690, Champaign, IL 61826. Send a self-addressed, stamped envelope. The directory includes over 400 telephone numbers worldwide of tourist boards.

For an updated list of states' tourist offices, send a self-addressed, stamped envelope to: Travel Industry Association of America, 1133 - 21st Street NW, Washington, D.C. 20036; and request a copy of *Discover America.*

State Tourist Board Offices

Alabama	800-252-2262 or 334-242-4169	Fax: 334-242-4554
Alaska	907-465-2010	Fax: 907-465-2287
Arizona	800-842-8257	Fax: 602-240-5475
	602-230-7733	
Arkansas	800-628-8725 or 501-682-7777	Fax: 501-682-1364
California	800-862-2543 or 916-322-2881	Fax: 916-322-3402
Connecticut	800-CTBOUND	Fax: 860-258-4275
	860-258-4355	
Delaware	800-441-8846 or 302-739-4271	Fax: 302-739-5749
District of		
Columbia	202-789-7000	Fax: 202-789-7037
Florida	904-487-1462	Fax: 904-921-9158
Georgia	404-656-3590	Fax: 404-651-9063
Hawaii	808-923-1811	Fax: 808-922-8991
Hawaii	808-961-5797 (Big Island)	
Kauai	808-245-3971	
Maui	808-244-3530	
Molokai	808-553-3876	
Oahu	808-923-1811	
Idaho	800-635-7820 or 208-334-2470	Fax: 208-334-2631
Illinois	800-2CONNECT for brochures	
	312-814-4732	Fax: 312-814-6175
	800-406-6918 terminal display for deaf	
Indiana	800-759-9191or 317-232-8860	Fax: 317-233-6887
Iowa	800-345-IOWAor 515-242-4705	Fax: 515-242-4749
Kansas	800-2KANSAS or 913-296-6988	Fax: 913-296-2009
Kentucky	800-225-TRIP or 502-564-4930	Fax: 502-564-5695
Louisiana	800-633-6970 or 504-342-8119	Fax: 504-342-8390
Maine	800-533-9595or 207-623-0363	Fax: 207-623-0388
Maryland	800-543-1036 for brochures	Fax: 410-333-6643
	410-767-3400	
Massachusetts	800-447-MASS for brochures	Fax: 617-727-6525
	617-727-3201	
Michigan	800-543-2YES or 517-373-0670	Fax: 517-373-0059
Minnesota	800-657-3700 or 612-296-5029	Fax: 612-296-7095
Mississippi	800-WARMEST; 601-359-3297	Fax: 601-359-5757
Missouri	800-877-123 or 573-751-4133	Fax: 573-751-5160
Montana	800-VISIT MT or 406-444-2654	Fax: 406-444-1800
Nebraska	800-228-4307 or 402-471-3796	Fax: 402-471-3026
Nevada	800-NEVADA-8 or 702-687-4322	Fax: 702-687-6779
New Hampshire	800-FUN-IN-NH or 603-271-2343	Fax: 603-271-6784
New Jersey	800-JERSEY-7 or 609-292-2470	Fax: 609-633-7418
New Mexico	800-545-2040 or 505-827-7402	Fax: 505-827-7400
New York	800-CALL-NYS or 518-474-4116	Fax: 518-486-6416

North Carolina	800-VISIT-NC or 919-733-4171	Fax: 919-733-8582
North Dakota	800-435-5663 or 701-328-2525	Fax: 701-328-4878
Ohio	800-BUCKEYE or 614-466-8844	Fax: 614-466-6744
Oklahoma	800-652-6552 or 405-521-3981	Fax: 405-521-3992
Oregon	800-547-7842 or 503-986-0000	Fax: 503-986-0001
Pennsylvania	800-VISIT-PA or 717-787-5453	Fax: 717-234-4560
Rhode Island	800-556-2484 or 401-277-2601	Fax: 401-273-8270
South Carolina	803-734-0122	Fax: 803-734-0133
South Dakota	800-S-DAKOTA or 605-773-3301	Fax: 605-773-3256
Tennessee	800-TENN-200 or 615-741-2158	Fax: 615-741-7225
Texas	800-452-9292	Fax: 512-483-3793
Utah	800-200-1160 or 801-538-1030	Fax: 801-538-1399
Vermont	800-VERMONT or 802-828-3237	Fax: 802-828-3233
Virginia	800-932-5827 or 804-786-2051	Fax: 804-786-1919
Washington	800-544-1800 or 360-586-2088/2102	
Washington, D.C.	See District of Columbia	
West Virginia	800-CALL-WVA or 304-558-2286	Fax: 304-558-0108
Wisconsin	800-432-TRIP or 608-266-2161	Fax: 608-266-3403
Wyoming	800-CALL-WYO or 307-777-7777	Fax: 307-777-6904

Cities, Counties, and Other Tourist Board Offices

Albuquerque, NM	800-284-2282		El Paso, TX	800-351-6024
Anchorage, AK	800-446-5352		Eureka, CA	800-346-3482
Atlanta, GA	800-ATLANTA		Everglades, FL	800-388-9669
Atlantic City, NJ	800-BOARDWALK		Fairbanks, AK	800-327-5774
Baltimore, MD	800-343-3468		Florida (Central)	800-828-7655
Boise, ID	800-635-5240		Florida (Keys)	800-872-3722
Charleston, WV	800-733-5469		Ft. Lauderdale, FL	800-356-1662
Charleston, SC	800-868-8118		Ft. Worth, TX	800-433-5747
Charlotte, NC	800-231-4636		Fredericksburg, VA	800-678-4748
Chattanooga, TN	800-322-3344		Galveston, TX	800-351-4237
Cheyenne, WY	800-246-5009			800-351-4236(TX)
Cincinnati, OH	800-344-3445		Green Bay, WI	800-236-3976
Cleveland, OH	800-321-1001		Greensboro, NC	800-344-2282
Colorado			Hartford, CN	800-446-7811
Springs, CO	800-DO-VISIT		Helena, MT	800-7-HELENA
Columbia, SC	800-264-4884		Houston, TX	800-365-7575
Columbia, OH	800-354-2657		Huntsville, AL	800-SPACE-4-U
Corpus Christi, TX	800-678-6232		Indianapolis, IN	800-323-INDY
Dallas, TX	800-752-9222		Ketchikan, AK	800-770-2200
Denver, CO	800-645-3446		Key Largo, FL	800-822-1088
Des Moines, IA	800-451-2625		Key West, FL	800-LAST-KEY
Detroit, MI	800-338-7648		Kissimmee, FL	800-831-1844
Durango Area, CO	800-525-8855		Knoxville, TN	800-727-8045

Kodiak, AK	800-789-4782	Providence, RI	800-233-1636
Lake Tahoe, CA	800-AT-TAHOE	Raleigh, NC	800-849-8499
Little Rock, AR	800-844-4781	Reno, NV	800-443-1482
Long Beach, CA	800-4LB-STAY	Richmond, VA	800-886-3705
Long Island, NY	800-441-4601	St. Louis, MO	800-916-0040
Los Angeles, CA	800-CATCH-LA	Salt Lake City, UT	800-541-4955
Louisville, KY	800-626-5646	San Antonio, TX	800-447-3372
	800-633-3384	San Jose, CA	800-SAN-JOSE
Memphis, TN	800-44-START	Santa Barbara, CA	800-927-4688
Miami, FL	800-933-8448	Santa Fe, NM	800-777-2489
Milwaukee, WI	800-231-0903	Sonoma	
Mississippi Gulf		County, CA	800-326-7666
Coast, MS	800-237-9493	South Padre	
Mobile, AL	800-566-2453	Island, TX	800-OK-PADRE
Myrtle Beach, SC	800-356-3016	Space Coast, FL	800-93-OCEAN
Newport		Tallahassee, FL	800-628-2866
Beach, CA	800-94-COAST	Taos County, NM	800-732-8267
New York		Temple	
City, NY	800-692-8474	Square, UT	800-453-3860,
Niagara Falls, NY	800-421-5223		ext. 4872
Oakland, CA	800-2-OAKLAND	Tulsa, OK	800-558-3311
Oklahoma		Utah Canyonlands	800-635-6622
City, OK	800-225-5652	Utah Canyonlands	
Omaha, NE	800-332-1819	Visitor Center	800-574-4FUN
Palm Springs, CA	800-347-7746	Utah's Dinosaur	
Park City, UT	800-453-1360	Land	800-477-5558
Pennsylvania		Vail, CO	800-525-3875
Dutch, PA	800-723-8824	Valley Forge, PA	800-441-3549
Philadelphia, PA	800-537-7676	Williamsburg, VA	800-368-6511
Pittsburgh, PA	800-359-0758	Wilmington, DE	800-422-1181
Pocono		Yellowstone	
Mountains, PA	800-722-9199	Teton, ID	800-634-3246

International Tourist Board Offices

Tourism and visitor bureaus are an excellent source of information. Maps, guides, destination literature, and good advice is available, usually free of charge. Information offices of many of the most popular tourist destinations are listed below. If your destination is not listed, call directory information for New York City (area code 212, followed by 555-1212) or Los Angeles (area codes 213 and 310, followed by 555-1212) and ask for the tourism office of that country. If you are still unable to find the tourism and visitor office, contact the embassy in Washington, D.C. (area code 202) and ask. All countries maintain a diplomatic office in Washington, D.C. Some countries do not staff tourism offices, however.

Many tourism bureaus staff several offices located in cities across the country. If you live in a major city, check your telephone directory for an office close to home.

Many countries offer a **visitor's card** to international travelers such as the *Great British Heritage Pass*, which allows admission to more than 500 castles, manor homes, gardens, museums, and other historical sites in England, Scotland, and Wales for just $35 for seven days, $50 for 15 days, or $75 for one month. *Scandinavian Travel Card* provides discounts throughout Scandinavia and Iceland. *Singapore Plus Card* gives discounts at over 150 shops, attractions, and restaurants. The *Caribbean Classic Card* lists over 1,000 discounts of 5-50 percent at restaurants, car rentals, tours and sightseeing, nightclubs, duty-free shops, and so on. There are similar type discount cards and offers all over the world. Ask the tourist board regarding their availability and where to buy them. In almost all cases, you must purchase them before leaving.

Country:	Telephone:	Country:	Telephone:
Argentina	213-930-0681	Northwest	
Aruba	800-TO-ARUBA	Territories	800-661-0788
Australia	310-229-4870	Nova Scotia	800-565-0000
Austria	212-944-6880	Ontario	800-ONTARIO
Anguilla	212-682-0435	Prince	
Antigua and		Edward Island	800-463-4PEI
Barbuda	305-381-6762	Quebec	800-363-7777
Bahamas	800-4-BAHAMAS	Saskatchewan	800-667-7191
Out Islands	800-688-4752	Yukon	403-667-5340
Barbados	800-221-9831	Caribbean Tourism	
Belgium	212-758-8130	Organization	212-682-0435
Belize	800-624-0686	Cayman Islands	305-266-2300
Bermuda	800-223-6106	Chile	800-825-2332
Bolivia	800-BOLIVIA	China, Peoples Rep.	818-545-7504/5
Bonaire	212-956-5911	Cook Islands	800-624-6250
British		Costa Rica	800-343-6332
Virgin Islands	800-835-8530	Cuba[52]	416-362-0700
Canada		Cúraçao	800-270-3350
Alberta	800-661-8888	Denmark	212-949-2333
	403-427-4321	Dominican	
British Columbia	800-663-6000	Republic	212-575-4966
	604-387-1642	Egypt	212-336-2570
Manitoba	800-665-0040	Falkland Islands	510-525-8846
	204-945-3777	Finland	212-949-2333
New Brunswick	800-561-0123	Fiji	800-YEA-FIJI
Newfoundland		France	212-838-7800
and Labrador	800-563-6353	French Guiana	212-838-7800

Germany	212-661-7174	Palau	202-624-7793
	416-968-1986	Panama	800-382-7262
Grand Bahama		Papua New Guinea	714-752-5440
Island	800-448-3386	Peru	800-854-0023
Greece	212-421-5777	Philippines	213-852-1901
Grenada	800-927-9554	Poland	212-338-9412
Guadeloupe	212-838-7855	Portugal	212-354-4403
Guam	800-US3-GUAM	Puerto Rico	800-223-6530
Guatemala	800-742-4529	Romania	212-697-6972
Haiti	212-697-9767	Russian Federation	212-758-1162
Hong Kong	310-208-4582	St. Kitts and Nevis	800-582-6208
Hungary	212-355-0240	St. Maarten (Dutch)	800-786-2278
Iceland	212-949-2333	St. Martin (French)	212-838-7855
India	212-586-4901	St. Lucia	800-456-3984
Indonesia	213-387-3089/2078	St. Vincent and the	
Israel	800-596-1199	Grenadines	800-729-1726
Italy	212-245-4822	Singapore	213-852-1901
Jamaica	800-233-4582	South Africa	800-222-5368
Japan	213-623-1952	Spain	212-265-8822
Jordan	212-949-0050	Sri Lanka	202-483-4025
Kenya	212-486-1300	Suriname	800-327-6864
Korea, South	800-868-7567	Sweden	212-949-2333
Luxembourg	212-935-8888	Switzerland	212-757-5944
Malaysia	213-689-9702	Tahiti and French	
Martinique	310-271-6665	Polynesia	310-414-8484
Micronesia,		Taiwan	415-989-8677/94
Federated States	800-348-0842	Thailand	213-382-2353
Mexico	800-44-MEXICO	Tonga	415-781-0365
	800-225-2786	Turkey	212-687-2194
	800-522-1516	Turks and Caicos	212-223-2323
	(AZ, CA, NV)	Trinidad and	
Baja (Norte)	800-225-2786	Tobago	800-748-4224
	800-522-1516	United Kingdom	
Los Cabos	800-765-CABOS	British Tourist	
Monaco	212-759-5227	Authority (BTA)	800-462-2748
Morocco	212-557-2520	Ireland	212-418-0800
Netherlands		Northern Ireland	800-326-0036
(Holland)	310-348-9339	U.S. Virgin Islands	212-332-2222
New Caledonia	310-271-6665	Vanuatu	800-677-4277
New Zealand	800-388-5494	Venezuela	212-826-1660
Norway	212-949-2333		

Rail Companies

The following is a list of popular rail companies with offices in North America. For areas not listed here, consult your travel agent. The information is accurate at the time of printing and subject to change without notice by the rail companies.

Alaska Railroad Corporation	800-544-0552	
Amtrak	800-USA-RAIL	
	800-523-8720	Metroliner Service
	800-523-6590	Hearing impaired
Australia Rail	800-423-2880	
	310-643-0032 (ATS Tours)	
BritRail	800-677-8585	
	Rail Passes: BritRail Classic Pass, BritRail Flexipass, BritRail Senior Pass, Free BritRail Kid's Pass	
Bulgarian State Railways	212-573-5530 (Balkan Holidays)	
CIT/Italian State Railways	800-223-7987 (except AK, HI, NY)	
	310-338-8616 Los Angeles	
	212-697-2100 New York City	
	Rail Passes: Italian Rail Pass, Italian Flexipass, Kilometric Pass, Eurail Pass, Eurail Silver, Eurail Youth Pass, German Pass	

Finnish State Railways	800-688-EURO (EuroCruises)
	800-677-6454 (Holiday Tours)
	800-233-SCAN (Scantours)
	800-848-6444 (Sea'n Air Travel)

GermanRail

Ticket Reservations: 800-782-2424*
Fax: 800-282-7474
310-479-2772 Los Angeles
Rail Pass Reservations: 800-782-2424 USA*
Rail Passes: Austrian Railpass, Benelux Tourrail
Pass, Copenhagen Pass, Eurail Flexipass, Eurailpass,
Eurailpass/Hertz Drive, Eurail Saverpass, Eurail
Youth Flexipass, Eurail Youth Pass, Eurolines Pass,
Europass, Europass/Hertz Drive (1st and 2nd class),
German Rail Hertz Drive, German Rail Twinpass,
German Rail Youth Pass, Greek Railpass, Holland
Pass, Italian Railpass, Norway Pass, Prague
Excursion Pass, ScanRail Pass, ScanRailpass/Hertz
Drive, ScanRail Senior 55+, Sweden Railpass

India Railway System

Information: 213-380-8855 Los Angeles
212-586-4901 New York City
Reservations: 212-997-3300
Fax: 212-997-3320
Rail Passes: Indrail Pass

Indonesia State Railways

213-387-2078 Information only

Irish Intercity Rail

800-243-7687
Rail Passes: Emerald Isle Card, ExplorerPass,
Rover Pass

Japan - Central
Japan Railway Co.

213-617-7353
Fax: 213-617-7464
Rail Passes: Japan Rail Pass

Japan - East
Japan Railway Co.

212-332-8686 Information only
Fax: 212-332-8690
For exchange order purchase, contact Japan Travel
Bureau International or Nippon Travel Agency
located in major cities in the United States and
Canada
Rail Passes: Japan Rail Pass

Japan - West
Japan Railway Co.

212-332-8686 Information only

Fax: 212-332-8690.
Rail Passes: Japan Rail Pass

Korea National Railroads

312-819-2560 Chicago, Information only
213-382-3435 Los Angeles, Information only

Malaysia and Singapore
KTM Berhad

213-689-9702 Information only
Rail Passes: KTYM Railpass

Sabah State
Railways

213-689-9702 Information only

Netherlands Railways

800-598-8501
Rail Passes: Benelux Tourrail Pass, Netherlands
Rail Pass.

New Zealand
Tranz Rail Ltd.

800-423-2880
Fax:310-643-0032

Polish State Railways

212-338-9412 Information only
800-223-6037 Ticket vouchers (Orbis)
Rail Passes: Polrail Pass

Rail Europe Inc.

800-4-EURAIL
Rail Passes: Austrian Pailpass, Benelux Junior,
Benelux Tourrail, Bulgarian Flexipass, Czech
Flexipass, EurailDrive Pass, Eurail Flexipass,
Eurailpass, Eurail Saverpass, Eurail Youth Flexipass,
Eurail Youthpass, Europass, Europass Youth,
Europass Drive, European East Pass, Finnrail
Flexipass, France Rail'N Drive, France Rail 'N Fly,
France Railpass, Hungarian Flexipass, Norway
Railpass, Portugese Railpass, Romanian Pass,
Scanrail 'N Drive, Scanrail Pass, Scan 55, Scanrail
Youth, Spain Flexipass, Spain Rail 'N Drive, Swiss
Card, Swiss Flexipass, Swiss Pass, Swiss Rail 'N
Drive

Romanian State Railways

212-697-6971 Information only

Russian State Railways

212-661-7913
Fax:212-661-7849

Russian Trans Siberian Road[53]	212-661-7913 Fax:212-661-7849
Spanish National Railway	800-222-8383
Swedish State Railways	800-782-2424* (DER Tours)
Sri Lanka Railway Service	202-483-4025 Information only
Taiwan Railway Administration	212-466-0691 New York City, Information only 312-346-1037 Chicago, Information only 415-989-8677 San Francisco, Information only
Thailand State Railway	212-432-0433 New York City, Information only 213-382-2353 Los Angeles, Information only
Turkish State Railways	312-311-0620
Ontario Northland	800-268-9281 (except area code 705) 800-461-8558 (area code 705)
Via Rail Canada	800-561-3949 * 800-561-8630 (AB, BC, MB, NT, ON area code 807, SK, YT) 800-561-3952 (NB, NS, PE); 800-561-3926 (NF) 800-361-1235 (ON area codes 519, 613, 705, 905) 800-361-5390 (PQ, except Montreal) 800-268-9503 (for hearing/speech impaired Canada, except Toronto)

* except AK, HI

Helpful Telephone Numbers

U.S. Airlines

Air Midwest	800-428-4322	Mahalo Air	800-462-4256
Air Nevada	800-634-6377	Midway	800-446-4392
Air South	800-247-7688	Midwest Express	800-452-2022
Air Virginia	800-446-7834	Mohawk	800-252-2144
AirTran Airways	800-247-8726	Nantucket	800-635-8787
Alaska	800-426-0333	Nations Air	800-248-9538
Aloha	800-367-5250	New England	800-243-2460
America West	800-235-9292	Northwest	800-225-2525
American	800-433-7300	Pacific Coastal	800-663-2872
American		Pan Am	888-267-2626
Trans Air	800-225-2995	Reno Air	800-736-6243
Arizona Airways	800-274-0662	Scenic	800-634-6801
Big Sky	800-237-7788	SkyWest	800-453-9417
Branson	800-442-4247	Southwest	800-435-9792
Cape Air	800-352-0714	Spirit	800-772-7117
Carnival	800-437-2110	Sun Country	800-359-5786
Comair	800-354-9822	Tower	800-221-2500
Continental	800-525-0280	TWA	800-221-2000
Delta	800-221-1212	United	800-241-6522
Frontier	800-432-1359	USAir	800-428-4322
Grand Airways	800-554-7263	Valujet	800-825-8538
Hawaiian	800-367-5320	Vanguard	800-826-4827
Horizon Air	800-547-9308	Western Pacific	800-930-3030
Kiwi International	800-538-5494	Wings West	800-252-0017
Lone Star	800-877-3932	World Airways	800-967-5350

Foreign Airlines

ACES	800-846-2237	Alitalia	800-223-5730
AOM French		ALM Antillean	800-327-7197
Airlines	800-892-9136	ANA - All Nippon	800-235-9262
Aer Lingus	800-223-6537	Ansett	800-366-1300
Aero California	800-237-6225	Asiana	800-227-4262
Aero Costa Rica	800-237-6247	Australian	800-448-9400
Aeroflot	800-995-5555	Austrian	800-843-0002
Aerolíneas		Avensa	800-428-3672
Argentinas	800-333-0276	Avianca	800-284-2622
Aeromar	800-950-0747	Bahamas	800-222-4262
Aeroméxico	800-237-6639	Balkan Bulgarian	800-852-0944
Aeroperu	800-777-7717	Baltic International	800-548-8181
Air Afrique	800-456-9192	British Airways	800-247-9297
Air Antillean	800-327-7230	British Midland	800-788-0555
Air Aruba	800-882-7822	BWIA	800-327-7401
Air Caledonie	800-677-4277	Cameroon Air	800-677-4277
Air Canada	800-776-3000	Canadian Air	
Air China (P.R.C.)	800-982-8802 (East)	International	800-426-7000
	800-986-1986 (West)	Cathay Pacific	800-233-2742
Air Fiji	800-677-4277	Cayman	800-441-3003
Air France	800-237-2747	China (R.O.C.)	800-227-5118
Air Guadeloupe	800-522-3394	China Eastern	800-200-5118
Air India	800-223-2250	Condor	800-524-6975
Air Inter	800-237-2747	Croatia	800-247-5353
Air Jamaica	800-523-5585	Cyprus	800-333-2977
Air Lanka	800-421-9898	Czech	800-223-2365
Air Littoral	800-237-2747	Dominicana	800-327-7240
Air Malta	800-756-2582	Dragon	800-233-2742
Air Marshall		East-West	800-354-7471
Islands	800-543-3898	Ecuatoriana	800-328-2367
Air Mauritius	800-537-1182	Egyptair	800-334-6787
Air Nauru	800-677-4277	El Al	800-223-6700
Air New Zealand	800-262-1234	Emirates	800-777-3999
Air Nuigini	714-752-5440	Ethiopian	800-445-2733
Air Pacific	800-227-4446	EVA	800-695-1188
Air Panama	800-272-6262	Faucett Peru	800-334-3356
Air Paraguay	800-677-7771	Finnair	800-950-5000
Air Seychelles	800-677-4277	Garuda	800-342-7832
Air UK	800-249-2478	Gulfstream	800-992-8532
Air Ukraine	800-857-2463	Gulf	800-553-2824
Air Vanuatu	800-677-4277	Guyana	800-242-4210
Air Zaire	800-442-5114	Iberia	800-772-4642
Air Zimbabwe	800-228-9485	Icelandair	800-223-5500
Alaska	800-426-0333	Indian	800-442-4455

Japan	800-525-3663	Royal Nepal	800-266-3725
Kenya	800-343-2506	Royal Tongan	800-486-6426
KLM	800-374-7747	Sabena	800-955-2000
Korean	800-438-5000	SAS	800-221-2350
Kuwait	800-458-9248	Saudi Arabian	800-472-8342
Lacsa Costa Rica	800-541-4243	Silk Air	800-745-5247
Ladeco	800-432-2799	Singapore	800-742-3333
LanChile	800-735-5526	Solomon	800-677-4277
Lauda	800-645-3880	South African	800-722-9675
Lloyd Aéreo		Suriname	800-327-6864
Boliviano	800-327-7407	Swissair	800-221-4750
LTU International	800-888-0200	TACA	800-535-8780
LOT Polish	800-223-0593	Taesa	800-848-2372
Lufthansa	800-581-6400	Tan Sasha	800-327-1225
Malaysia	800-421-8641	TAP Air Portugal	800-221-7370
Malev Hungarian	800-223-6884	Thai International	800-426-5204
Martinair Holland	800-627-8462	Transbrasil	800-262-1706
Mexicana	800-531-7921	Trans-Jamaican	800-263-4354
Middle East	800-664-7310	Turkish	800-874-8875
Mount Cook	800-468-2665	Turks and Caicos	800-845-2161
NICA	800-831-6422	Varig	800-468-2744
Olympic	800-223-1226	VASP Brazilian	800-732-8277
Pakistan		Viasa International	800-892-8898
International	800-221-2552	Vietnam	800-565-2742
Philippine	800-435-9725	Virgin Atlantic	800-862-8621
Polynesian	800-644-7659	Yemen	800-382-4484
Qantas	800-227-4500	Yugoslav	800-752-6528
Royal Air Maroc	800-344-6726	Zambia	800-223-1136
Royal Jordanian	800-223-0470		

Airline Consumer Relations Offices

Some numbers will connect you directly with the Customer Relations Department, others will connect you with Reservations and you may ask to be transferred. You may call the Reservation Department of any airline, cruise line, hotel, and/or car rental company and ask for their Customer Relations telephone number.

Aer Lingus	800-322-7873	Korean	310-417-5200
Air Canada	800-366-0362	Lufthansa	800-645-3880
Air France	800-872-3224	Mexicana	800-353-8245
Air New Zealand	800-262-2468	Midway	800-564-5001
Alaska	800-426-0333	Midwest Express	800-452-2022
Alitalia	800-903-9991		ext. 3910
America West	800-235-9292	Northwest	612-726-2046
American	817-967-2000	Polynesian	800-644-7659
American		Qantas	310-726-1407
Trans Air	800-225-2995	Reno Air	702-686-3835
Austrian	718-670-8600	SAS	800-345-9684
British Airway	800-422-9101	Singapore	213-934-8833
Canadian		Southwest	214-904-4223
International	403-569-4180	Swissair	800-221-4750
Carnival	305-923-8672	Thai	
Cathay Pacific	310-640-8551	International	800-426-5204
Continental	800-932-2732	Tower Air	718-556-4300
Delta	404-715-1450		ext. 289
El Al	212-852-0600	TWA	800-221-2000
Eva Air	310-521-6000	United Airlines	708-952-6796
Finnair	800-950-4768	USAir	910-661-0061
Iberia	305-267-7747	Valujet	800-825-8538
Icelandair	410-715-1600	Virgin Atlantic	800-496-6661
Japan	800-525-3663		
Kiwi			
International	201-645-1133		

Car Rental Companies

Company	Telephone	Market
Alamo	800-462-5266	United States and Europe
Auto Europe	800-223-5555	Europe
Avis	800-331-1212	United States
	800-331-1084	International
Budget	800-527-0700	United States
	800-472-3325	International
DER Tours	800-782-2424	Europe
Dollar	800-800-4000	United States
	800-800-6000	International
Enterprise	800-325-8007	United States
Hertz	800-654-3131	United States
	800-654-3001	International
Holiday Autos	800-422-7737	Europe
Kemwel	800-678-0678	Europe
Kenning	800-227-8990	Europe
National	800-227-7368	United States
	800-227-3876	International
Payless	800-237-2804	United States
Thrifty	800-367-2277	United States
Ugly Duckling	800-843-3825	United States
U-Save	800-438-2300	United States
Value	800-327-2501	United States

For international rentals, contact the national tourist board of the country or countries you plan to visit and ask for a vacation planner. Some provide these useful guides, some do not. If you receive a vacation planner, local car rental companies based in that country are often listed. Whenever paying for an international rental in a foreign currency, read the contract carefully. Watch out for add-ons and taxes. Whenever possible, reserve a car that is payable in U.S. dollars.

Recommended Reading

This is both an easy and a difficult section to write. Easy because there are so many good travel books, guides, magazines, and periodicals. Difficult, for the very same reason. The list is purposively brief; you can add to or take away from it. Inasmuch as there are tens of thousands of books on individual countries, continents, and special interests, I have chosen to avoid, in most cases, reference to a specific destination guide book, but recommend a guide book series. Listings are alphabetical, not ranked in order.

Favorite Travel Magazines:

> *Condé Nast Traveler*
> *Explorer*
> *Islands*
> *National Geographic Traveler*

Favorite Travel Guide Books:

Blue Book. Well written and documented guide to European countries and cities. Very comprehensive and detailed. Published by W.W. Norton.

Culture Shock! Interesting and informative guide to customs and etiquette of various countries. Practical advice is given regarding social customs, business dealings, communication, food and cuisine, language, gestures, host expectations, entertaining, etc. Published by Graphic Arts Center Publishing Company.

Frommer's. Arthur Frommer, the dean of travel writers! His travel guide books are easy to read and packed with information. Destination guide books are written by different authors and some books are better than others. As a group, though, they're pretty good. There are different publishers for the various books.

***Lonely Planet* series.** These well written guide books cover almost every corner of the world. Published by Lonely Planet Publications.

Michelin Tourist Guide. The city guides are particularly good. If I could only pick one city guide, it would be Michelin. Country guide books are also available. Published by Michelin Travel Publications.

Favorite Cultural Reading:

Culturgrams. An in-depth review, commentary, and analysis of the culture, customs, and people of individual countries. At present, 153 *Culturgram* publications are available. These booklets are among the best studies on travel and culture I have seen. *Culturgrams* are not a sightseeing guide book, but a practical guide to understanding the country, its customs, and the people that you will be visiting. Each report is four pages and contains information regarding land and climate, history, population, language, religion, general attitudes, personal appearance, customs and courtesies, greetings, gestures, visiting, eating, lifestyle, family, dating and marriage, diet, recreation, holidays, commerce, government, economy, transportation and communication, education, and health. I consider *Culturgrams* a "must read" for my travels.

Published by Brigham Young University, *Culturgrams* are available in both printed form and CD-ROM. A complete set of 153 printed *Culturgrams* is only $115 plus postage and handling. Individual printed copies are available for $4.50 plus shipping and handling. A discount is provided for purchases of more than one copy of individual reports.

For printed copies, contact:
    Brigham Young University
    David M. Kennedy Center for International Studies, Publications
    P.O. Box 24538
    Provo, UT 84602-4538
    Telephone: 800-528-6279 or 801-378-3377
    Fax: 801-378-5882
For CD-ROM version, contact:
    Microsoft Inc.
    Telephone: 800-376-5125

Another favorite reference and reading source is ***Background Notes***, published by the U.S. State Department and includes history, maps, and other pertinent information regarding individual countries. Available through:

Superintendent of Documents
U.S. Government Printing Office
P.O. Box 371954
Pittsburgh, PA 15250-7954

Just A Few Other Favorites for Reading:

America's Most Charming Towns and Villages. Open Road Publishing.

Europe 101. Rick Steves and Gene Openshaw. John Muir Publications. An easy and practical guide and explanation of European art history which helps travelers understand and appreciate their sightseeing.

Mona Wink's. Rick Steves and Gene Openshaw. John Muir Publications. Self-guided tours of Europe's top museums. Rick Steve has authored many well written travel guide books.

The National Trust Guide to Historic Bed and Breakfasts. John Wiley and Sons Publishing.

Off The Beaten Path. A guide to more than 1,000 scenic, quaint, and interesting places that are not tourist meccas, but are off the beaten track. Published by The Reader's Digest Association.

100 Best Family Resorts in North America. Tice and Wilford. Globe Pequot Publishing.

Recommended Country Inns. Globe Pequoit Publishing.

The World's Best - The Ultimate Book for the International Traveler. Kathleen Peddicord, ed., Agora Inc., publisher. This is a fun book which lists the best of everything that 30 countries and continents have to offer.

Footnotes

[1] Sometimes special promotional fares during a fare war are excluded for coupon discounts. Always read the terms, conditions, and rules completely and carefully.

[2] Source: Airport Council International. *Parade;* October 20, 1996; page 22.

[3] Read Chapter Four on travel clubs. An aggressive, legitimate travel club will not only keep you informed of the best travel bargains, discount offers, promotions, etc., but save you hundreds and/or thousands of dollars in the process.

[4] The fares listed here and in other places are valid at the time of printing. Airfares are constantly changing and the rates may be higher or lower when you want to travel. These fares illustrate my point that one should *always* check alternate cities.

[5] Delta Air Lines (LR1COMN). The first passenger pays $218 and the second passenger, or companion flies free. The average fare is only $109 per person.

[6] I have used examples where there is no non-stop service. Breaking the fare may work in any situation regardless if there is non-stop service. Some travelers are willing to pay a premium for non-stop. I will pay a *little* more to avoid connections, but not an arm and a leg! Non-stop service will have a different value to each traveler, but as for me and my house, we will save the money!

[7] *Business Travel News/BTN;* October 28, 1996; page 4.

[8] *Travel & Leisure;* October 1996; page 126. It is interesting to note that Midwest Express was rated #1 by the readers of *Condé Nast Traveler,* but did not receive a rat-

ing in the *Travel & Leisure* survey. My guess is that Midwest Express, a regional carrier, probably did not appear in the *Travel & Leisure* survey and therefore received no rating.

[9]*Condé Nast Traveler*, October 1996; page 210.

[10]See *USA Today*, September 13, 1996, page 6E.

[11]Source: Official Airlines Guide survey of 2,266 international business travelers from the United States, Great Britain, France, Germany, Hong Kong, and Singapore. *Travel Weekly*; September 9, 1996; page 71.

[12]*Travel Weekly*; July 25, 1996; page 13.

[13]*U.S. Travel Agency Survey;* August 29, 1996; page 166.

[14]Costa Cruises also offers Super Senior Rates, Costa Kid Rates, and Suite Deals.

[15]Crystal's Advance Booking Rate is not to be confused with an early booking discount, which Crystal also offers. Advance Booking Rates, which typically offer discounts of 5-30 percent off the brochure rate can be booked right up to your sailing date. Crystal's Guaranteed Group Rate differs from other cruise lines' guaranteed group fares in that Crystal's can only be booked through a travel club, travel agency, association, or consortium that has been appointed by Crystal to offer these special discounts. Typically, the Guaranteed Group Rate on Crystal Cruises will offer an additional 10 percent discount below the Advance Booking Rate yielding up to a 40 percent discount. Crystal also offers a repeat customer discount of five percent called a Crystal Society discount. Want the lowest cruise fare? Book a Guaranteed Group Rate at 40 percent off; an early booking discount of five percent; an early payment discount of 10 percent; and a Crystal Society member discount of five percent. That's a 60 percent discount off the brochure rate! That's how to *Shop Smart!*

[16]Cunard's Multiple Rates are only available through specially appointed travel clubs, travel agencies, associations, and consortiums. The discount typically runs 5-30 percent depending on the sailing. Cunard also offers special promotion rates on selected sailings and an early booking discount.

[17]"Saver" is appended to the geographic itinerary of the cruise, i.e., European Savers, Caribbean Savers, Alaska Savers, etc.

[18]Norwegian Caribbean Line.

[19]Leadership Fares are the lowest rates offered by NCL, with the exception of ad hoc promotions. When you book a Run of the Ship Fare, you select a sailing date and your cruise ship. You are guaranteed a cabin on that cruise sailing. NCL will assign your stateroom. It could be a suite or a minimum cabin. You are guaranteed a cabin, but are not guaranteed, at the time of booking, your cabin category, deck, sleeping accommodations (one queen bed, two double beds, upper and lower berths), etc.

[20]Premier Cruise Lines (the "Big Red Boat") does not offer a standard discount program, but does offer, on a regular basis, individual promotions and discounts, typically around a $100 per person. Some sailings will offer even better discounts. One of the most popular premier discounts is their "Kids Cruise and Vacation Free" promotion.

Two years ago I took my family, all seven of us, on the Big Red Boat. The cruise, which features the Looney Tunes characters, is one of the best family vacations. Combine Premier's three or four-day cruise with a stay in Orlando. It's a tough act to follow!

[21]Radisson does not provide a standard discount program, but does offer special promotions and discounts on selected sailings. You remember the key? You got it...Always ask!

[22]RCCL, Royal Caribbean Cruises Ltd.

[23]Seabourne Cruises offers a wide variety of promotions and rate reductions on their sailings. (Seabourne does not offer "discounts," but they do offer "reductions." I don't care what they want to call it as long as I save money...As for me and my house, I'll call it a discount!) These include:

Early Payment Reduction: five percent discount if you pay six months in advance; 10 percent discount if you pay one year in advance.

Share Reductions: When two cabins are booked either by passengers traveling together or by the booking agency, for the same sailing. Discount (pardon me, "reduction") runs from $200 to $2,000 per person. If cabins are booked by an agency, the agency should look for passengers traveling on the same cruise so that they both can get a "reduction." Passengers need only be booked on the same cruise, but don't need to travel "together."

Seabourne Club: 10 percent discount (yeah, I know) available to all persons who have previously sailed with Seabourne.

Seabourne Club Awards: Discounts offered as a result of your previous cumulative sailing days with Seabourne. After you have sailed a cumulative total of 28 days, you receive a 25 percent discount on a future cruise of 14 days or less; after 70 days, a 50 percent discount; and after 1,409 days, you receive a free cruise of 14 days or less.

Collectors Cruise Savings: 10-50 percent discount when you book back-to-back cruises.

Grand Cruises Rates: specially priced cruises.

Seasonal Rates: Discounts offered for selected sailings, including repositioning cruises. Discount varies with each sailing, but can reach 50 percent off.

World Fares: Creative concept for cruise lovers. You purchase 45, 60, 90, or 120 cruise days aboard your choice of sailings. You have three years from the date of your first World fares cruise to use your cruise days. The per diem costs are the lowest offered by Seabourne.

[24]*1996-1997 RCCL Caribbean and Bahamas* brochure, page 54.

[25]Rates for the suites have not been included.

[26]Princess Cruises 1997 *Alaska and Canadian Rockies* brochure, pages 29, 88-91.

[27]*Travel Weekly;* August 29, 1996; page 13.

[28]*Travel & Leisure;* October 1996; page 125.

[29]*Condé Nast Traveler;* October 1996; page 210.

[30]*Travel Weekly;* October 7, 1996; page 60.

[31]*USA Today;* March 1, 1996; page 3E. India was added by me!

[32]Kiwi International has filed for Chapter 11 Bankruptcy Protection as this book goes to press.

[33]Source: U.S. Department of Transportation. *USA Today;* October 21, 1996; page 1B. For period January - June, 1996.

[34]Source: U.S. Department of Transportation. *USA Today;* October 18, 1996; page 1B. For period January - June, 1996.

[35]Source: U.S. Department of Transportation. *USA Today;* October 21, 1996; page 1B. For period January - June, 1996.

[36]*Robert Louis Stevenson In the South Seas*, Alanna Knight, ed. Paragon House Publishers, New York. 1987. Page 36.

[37]International Bonded Couriers (I.B.C.).

[38]*Travel Weekly*; September 12, 1996; page 25.

[39]Official Airlines Guide survey of 2,266 international business travelers in the United States, Europe, and Asia. *Travel Weekly*; August 19, 1996; page 33.

[40]*Travel Weekly*; August 15, 1996; page 19.

[41]*Ibid.*

[42]Survey conducted by Sea World/Busch Gardens at theme parks. *Travel Weekly*, August 5, page 57.

[43]*Amusement Business* magazine, Nashville, TN. Attendance figures are estimates. Ibid.

[44]Ibid.; April 8, 1996; page 31.

[45]Source: CLT Research Associates and Marriott Lodging International. *Business Travel News*; October 14, 1996; page 12.

[46]Source: CLT Research Associates and MarriottLodging International. *Business Travel News*; October 14, 1996; page 12.

[47]U.S. Travel Agency Survey; August 29, 1996; page 62.

[48]*Travel Weekly*; May 20, 1996; page 33.

[49]Source: U.S. Department of Transportation. *Travel Weekly*; April 8, 1996; page 31.

[50]Southwest Airlines does not have interline luggage agreement with other carriers. This decreases the chances of luggage being mishandled, although it is inconvenient for passengers making connections to other carriers who must retrieve their luggage from Southwest and re-check it with their connecting carrier.

[51]Source: U.S. Department of Transportation. *Travel Weekly*; May 13, 1996; page 59. DOT report shows airport on-time arrival and departure performance for 1995.

[52]At present, travel to Cuba is restricted for U.S. citizens.

[53]Must reading for all travelers interested in the trans-Siberian railway is *The Trans-Siberian Rail Guide*, Robert Strauss, Compass Publications. Distributed by Hunter Publishing; Edison, NJ.

Index

AARP, 98
ADA room, 7
Add-on fare, 7
Airport Code, 7, 36
Airports
  Busiest, 20
  On-time, 143
Airline affinity card, 8, 41-44
Airline tickets, 17-51
  Alternate cities, 24-28
  Back-to-back ticketing, 8, 28-30
  Bereavement fares, 36
  Breaking the fare, 8, 30-32
  Children's fares, 36, 38
  Coach fare, 9, 33
  Compassion fares, 9, 36
  Consolidator, 9, 22-24
  Delta Fantastic Flyer, 38
  Discount coupons, 20-22, 25-26, 99-101
  Kids Fly Free, 38
  International passes, 33-35
  Internet sales, 47-49
  Point beyond fares, 32-33
  Promotions, 20-22, 38-39
  Segment, 15
  Senior citizen, 36, 97-103
  Special circumstance, 36
  Special promotions, 20-22
  Split ticketing, 15, 30-32
  Stand-by, 15, 38, 101, 121
  Student fares, 38-40
  Through fare, 15
  Unpublished fare, 15
  Upgrade, 15, 49
  Youth fares, 38-40
Airlines
  Complaints, 39
  Consumer Relations, 180
  Busiest routes, 139-140
  Frequent Flyer programs, 11, 40-47,
    151-163
  Lost luggage, 36, 142
  Supervisor, 15
  Telephone numbers, 177-179
  Wine selection in-flight, 134
  World's best, 37
Alternate cities, 24-28
American Plan (AP), 7
AMTRAK, 109-110, 173
APEX, 7
ARTA, 21
ASTA, 21
ATO, 7

Back-to-back ticketing, 8, 28-30
Bed and breakfast, 87-88
Blackout dates, 8
Boarding pass, 8
Breaking the fare, 8, 30-32
BritRail Pass, 106, 113-144, 173

Bulk fare, 8
Bulkhead, 8
Bumping, 8, 120-124
Bus, 115
Business Class, 8

Cancellation penalty, 8
Capacity controlled, 8
Car Rentals, 89-95, 181
  Airline rates, 89
  Association rates, 89
  CDW, 9, 91-92
  Corporate rates, 89
  Counter shopping, 91
  Credit card coverage, 91-92
  Drop-off fee, 11
  International, 92-94, 114-115
  International Driver's License, 93
  Lost Revenue Liability, 92
  One-way rentals, 90
  Senior rates, 89
  Telephone numbers, 93
  Travel clubs, 89
  Upgrades, 90
CARP, 98
CDW, 9, 91-92
City pair, 9
CLIA, 21
Columbus Travel Club, 60-61
Coach Class, 9
Code share, 9
Commuter carrier, 9
Companion fare, 9
Concierge, 9
Configuration, 9
Connection, 9
Consolidator, 9, 22-24, 75
Continental breakfast, 10
Continental plan, 10
Corporate rate, 10
Courier travel, 125-131
Credit cards, 8, 40-44, 91-92
CRS, 10
Cruises, 63-76, 118

Air/Sea option, 71-72
Cabin selection, 65-66
Cancellation insurance, 67
Code words, 69-71
Consolidators, 75
Cruise only rates, 71-72
Dining, 66
Discount coupons, 72
Discounts, 63-72
Freighter, 73-75
Guaranteed discounts, 69
Guaranteed group rates, 69
Itinerary, 65
Personality match, 64, 67
Pre- and post- stays, 68, 73
Private rates, 69, 71
Shore excursions, 67-68
Terms and Conditions, 63, 66
Unpublished rates, 69
Upgrades, 66
World's best, 73
CTC, 10
CTO, 10
Culturgrams, 184

Debit memo, 10
Denied Boarding, 10, 120-124
Denied Boarding Compensation, 10, 120-124
Dining programs, 44
Direct flight, 11
Discount coupons, airline, 19, 20-21
Double booking, 11
Double dip, 19
Down line, 11
Double occupancy, 11
Drop-off fee, 11

Eurailpass, 111-113, 174, 175
Eurobus, 115-116
European Plan (EP), 11
Excursion fare, 11

Fare basis, 11
Fare wars, 18-19

FIM, 11
FIT, 11
Footnotes, 187-192
Freighter cruises, 73-75
Frequent Flyer programs, 11, 40-47, 61,
   151-163
   Credit cards, 40-47
   Elite status, 45-47

Gate agent, 12
Gateway city, 12
GEM, 81

Hidden-city ticketing, 12
Hotels, 73, 77-88
   Affinity discounts, 84
   Bed and breakfast, 87-88
   Consolidators, 9, 80-81
   Corporate rates, 10, 84-85
   Discount books, 81-82
   Discounts, 79-80, 84-85
   Europe, 82, 86-87
   Free discount magazines, 83
   Frequent Flyer mileage, 40-47
   Frequent Guest programs, 165-166
   International discount books, 82
   Negotiate your own rate, 77-79, 82-83
   Newspapers, 83
   Script, 83-84
   Senior discounts, 84
   Single supplement, 15
   Travel clubs, 59, 82
   University and college dorms, 85-86
   Vouchers, 83-84
   Weekend rates, 85
   Youth Hostels, 86
Hostels, 86, 105
Hub, 12
Hub and spoke, 12

IATAN card, 56
Incentive travel, 12
Inclusive rate, 12
Interline agreement, 12
Interline connection, 12
International airline passes, 33-35

International Driver's License, 93
Internet sales, 47-49
Involuntary denied boarding, 10

Japan Rail Pass, 116, 174
Joint fare, 12

Last minute sales, 47-49, 57-59
Leg, 12
Load factor, 13, 120

Manifest, 13, 125
Meeting fare/rate, 13
Midweek (X), 13
Modified American Plan (MAP), 13

No show, 13, 91

Occupancy rate, 13
Open jaw, 13
Option date, 13
Overbooking, 13, 120-121

PAI, 13
PEC, 13
PFC, 13
Pitch, 14
PNR, 14
Point beyond fare, 14, 32-33
Positive space, 14
Promotions, airline, 20-22, 38-39
Published fare, 14

Rack rate, 14
Rebate, 14
Recommended reading, 183-185
Restricted ticket, 14, 28-30
Resource library, 21
Rule 240, 14
Run-of-House (ROH), 14
Run-of-Ship (ROS), 14
Season, 14
Segment, 15
Self catering, 15
Senior Citizen Discounts, 36, 89, 97-
   107

AARP, 98
Airline coupon books, 99-101
Airline discounts, 99-103
Associations, 98
CARP, 98
Freedom Passport, 101-102
Global Passport, 102
Grandchildren, travel with, 105
Hotels, 84, 104-105
International airlines, 104
National parks, 105-106
Rental cars, 89, 104
Trains, 106-107
Single supplement, 15
Split ticketing, 15
Stand-by, 15, 38, 101, 121
Special circumstance travel, 36
Bereavement, 36
Compassion, 36
Senior, 36, 99-103, 104
Supervisor, 15

Theme parks, 137
Through fare, 15, 32-33
Ticketing deadline, 19
Top Tier Quick Qualifying, 47
Tour conductor passes, 118-119
Tour escorts, 118-119
Tourist offices, 167-172
International, 170-172
Local, 169-170
State, 168-169
Trains, 106, 109-116, 173-176
AMTRAK, 106, 109-110
BritRail, 106, 113-114, 173
Eurailpass, 106, 111-112, 174, 175
Europe, 106, 110-114, 173-176
Great Britain, 106, 113-114, 173
Japan Rail Pass, 116, 174
List of companies, 106, 173-176
Steam trains, 110
Travel agents, 21-22
CTC, 21
Gender of , 140-141
Resource library, 21

Specialist, 21
Travel clubs, 53-61
Membership checklist, 59-60
Travel Connections, 60-61
Travel Show, see Introduction

Unpublished fare, 15
Unrestricted ticket, 15, 28-30, 33
Upgrade, 15. 49, 90

Value Added Tax, 15
Voluntary denied boarding, 10, 120-121

Wait list, 15, 121
Waiver, 15
Weekend (W), 15

XANADU Enterprises, 118

Yield management, 58, 120
Youth fares, 38-40

To order additional copies of *Insider Secrets To Killer Travel Deals*

Write:
P.O. Box 22617
Salt Lake City, UT 84122-2617

Telephone: 800-373-3328